YORK
in the 1970s
A Decade That Changed a City

PAUL CHRYSTAL

AMBERLEY

First published 2016

Amberley Publishing
The Hill, Stroud
Gloucestershire, GL5 4EP

www.amberley-books.com

British Library Cataloguing in Publication Data.
A catalogue record for this book is available from the British Library.

ISBN 978 1 4456 4066 2 (print)
ISBN 978 1 4456 4098 3 (ebook)

Origination by Amberley Publishing.
Printed in Great Britain.

CONTENTS

INTRODUCTION

This is the third volume in a unique, exciting and revealing new series on the history of York, the first two of which, *York in the 1950s* and *York in the 1960s*, have already been published. As I said in the introduction to these earlier books, of the many books published on the fascinating and exhilarating history of York none, until this series emerged, focuses on what was happening here in one particular decade. *York in the 1970s* is, as the title suggests, an account of York life between 1970 and 1979.

The 1970s carry a lot of baggage in the nation's collective memory. It is often remembered as the decade in which the lights went out, or the decade that fashion forgot. Why would you want to remember the bombs of the IRA, endless strikes, Austin Allegros, flares and loons and space-hoppers? You wouldn't, but perhaps you should, because only then will memories of your foreign package holidays, a Blue Nun cooling in the fridge, David Bowie on the record player, 'Bohemian Rhapsody' on the colour TV, *Star Wars* on at the pictures, and Concorde flying rich people to Bahrain and New York – only then will your personal memories come flooding back. The 1970s enjoy something of a bad press, but they weren't all bad.

For York, it was a decade of famous anniversaries and consolidation after the visionary Esher Report and the centuries' delay in the opening of the University of York. Now was the time to start realising some of the Esher proposals and to allow York Civic Trust, the Georgian Society, YAYAS, York Archaeological Trust and other agencies to get on with preserving, conserving and equipping York for the twenty-first century and beyond. An early sign of good things to come was the pedestrianisation of Stonegate – that jewel of European streets – 'literally paving the way for the preservation and conservation of much of what we can still see and enjoy in York today, one of Europe's finest cities'. Crucial restoration of the Minster was completed, and York Archaeological Trust got to work methodically and meticulously excavating the city's Viking heritage and reaffirming its place as one of, if not the, country's centre for all things Norse. Similar recognition came with the opening of the enduringly awe-inspiring National Railway Museum, making York *the* place to visit for anyone looking for an interactive and tangible picture of our rich railway heritage. The smell alone, so redolent of the age of steam, makes a visit worthwhile. Three major anniversaries came round in the decade: in 1971, the 1900th anniversary of the foundation of Eboracum – Roman York – and the 500th anniversary of York Minster in the same year; in 1975, it was the 50th anniversary of Joseph Rowntree's death.

Indeed, the 1970s was a decade that defines York. If you had to pick three things that characterised the city, then Romans, Vikings and the Minster would be top of most lists. Add to that the canonization of Margaret Clitherow, the rehabilitation of George Hudson,

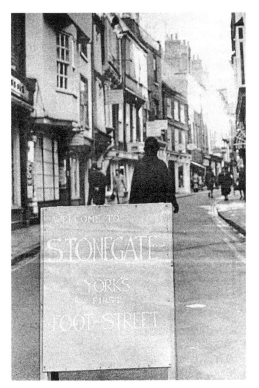
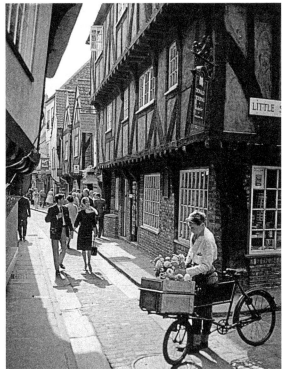

Above left: Paving the way for pedestrianisation.

Above right: Seventies shambles.

Railway King, the opening of the National Railway Museum, the anniversary of the death of Joseph Rowntree and the sell-off of Terry's and you have a decade in which all the important facets of York life and its heritage came together. The 1970s was indeed a decade that changed our city.

York in the 1970s explores and illuminates all of this and more. It will delight anyone who has sat in the dark playing cards to the guttering light of a candle, and for a change, talking to their parents. Anyone who has whiled their early life away listening to 'Dark Side of the Moon', 'Band on the Run' or 'Tubular Bells' on repeat, who has been scared witless by *The Exorcist* or who lived it up in Magaluf will engage with and love this book. To paraphrase what I said in my earlier decade books, 'It will have appeal, give pleasure and satisfy curiosity whether you grew up in York in the 1970s, whether you have left and want to rekindle your childhood and teenage memories, or whether you are just a child of the 1970s and are curious to know what you missed here. *York in the 1970s* will entertain, fascinate and inform with its facts, rarely seen photographs and its sheer, unadulterated nostalgia'.

Paul Chrystal, York, October 2016
paul.chrystal@btinternet.com

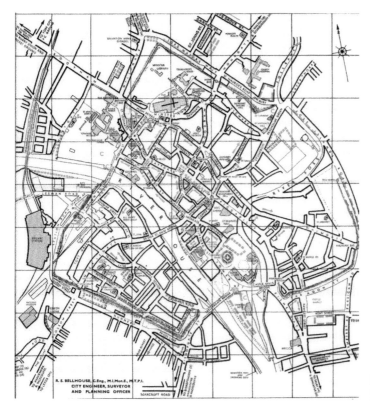

Map of York in the 1970s.

1970s Timeline

18 June 1970
Conservatives win the general election by 330 seats to Labour's 287. An unexpected result that reflected doubts about Labour's economic management.

1971
Stonegate in York pedestrianised.
The 1900th anniversary of the foundation of Eboracum – Roman York.
The 500th anniversary of York Minster.
York officially forgave the charlatan 'Railway King' George Hudson, restoring Railway Street to its earlier name of George Hudson Street.

6 February 1971
The first British soldier, Gunner Robert Curtis (aged twenty), was killed in Northern Ireland's 'Troubles' by the IRA while on foot patrol in North Belfast. British troops had been sent to the province in 1969 in a 'limited operation' to restore law and order.

15 February 1971
The old sterling denominations of pounds, shillings and pennies were phased out over a period of eighteen months. This decimalisation was blamed for an increase in inflation.

28 June 1971
York is host to the state visit of Queen Elizabeth II.

20 August 1971
The discovery of oil under the North Sea was a boost to British public finances. Drilling and exploration concessions were auctioned to maximise government income, and the

first oil was piped ashore at Teesside in 1975. Full-scale exploitation of the fields did not begin until the 1980s, when rising oil prices made it economically viable.

1972
Cosmopolitan magazine launched.

30 January 1972
The British Army shoots dead fourteen in Londonderry, Northern Ireland, on Bloody Sunday; the ramifications rumble on today.

4 August 1972
Idi Amin expels Uganda's Asians; many had the right to settle in Britain. Amin gave his country's Asian population ninety days to get out, claiming God had told him in a dream to do it. Over half of the 55,000 Asians expelled from Uganda came to Britain and many settled permanently, their resettlement a success story. In 1991, President of Uganda Yoweri Museveni invited them to 'return home' to help the Ugandan economy.

1 January 1973
Britain joins the European Economic Community.

1975
National Railway Museum opens in York. The 50th anniversary of Joseph Rowntree's death.
Skeldergate Bridge was opened for the last time. Its workings have since been removed.

May 1976
York Archaeological Trust begins its Coppergate Viking excavations.

September 1976
Britain is forced to borrow money from the International Monetary Fund.

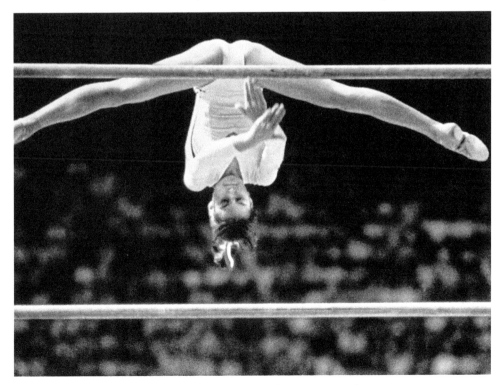

Nadia Comaneci on the asymmetrical bars, Montreal Olympics 1976.

25 July 1978

The world's first test-tube baby is born in Oldham. Louise Brown, the first 'test-tube baby', was a success for 'in vitro' fertilisation (IVF). By the end of the twentieth century, around 1,400 IVF babies were being born each year.

Winter 1978/79

Strikes paralyse Britain during the so-called Winter of Discontent: industrial action by petrol tanker and lorry drivers was followed by hospital ancillary staff, ambulance men and dustmen going on strike. Hospitals were picketed, the dead left unburied and troops called in to control rats swarming around heaps of uncollected rubbish.

1 March 1979

Scotland and Wales reject devolution.

3 May 1979

Conservative Margaret Thatcher becomes Britain's first female prime minister on the promise that the Conservatives would cut income tax, reduce public expenditure, make it easier for people to buy their own homes and curb the power of the unions.

27 August 1979

IRA killed the Queen's cousin Lord Mountbatten, one of his teenage grandsons and two others with a bomb on his boat at Mullaghmore in County Sligo, Ireland. On the same day, the IRA also killed eighteen soldiers at Warrenpoint in County Down.

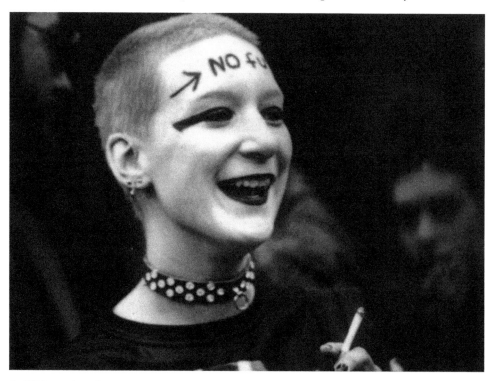

A 1970s punk rocker.

1

1970S BRITAIN

The 'swinging sixties' get credit for many things – in reality, some of them are myths: the mini (car) was launched at the end of the 1950s; the mini (skirt) was, sadly, nowhere near as ubiquitous as some 'remember'; the contraceptive pill only really took off for many women in the 1970s; and women only started to liberate themselves in the 1970s too, soon after the launch of *Spare Rib* in 1972 (W. H. Smith refused to stock it, but it sold 20,000 copies a month anyway). The 1970 publication of 'get a life' and Germaine Greer's *The Female Eunuch*, love it or loathe it, had a massive impact.

In some ways the 1960s were very restricting and restrictive: we had to go to court before we were allowed to read a book about a gamekeeper and a posh woman; we locked up a Rolling Stone for having a travel sickness tablet or two in his pocket, flabbergasting

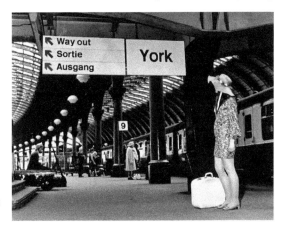

Mini-skirted girl on York railway station in 1969.

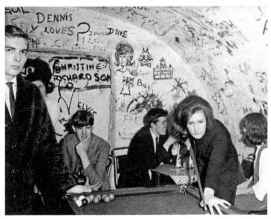

York's Kavern Club in 1964.

even the Archbishop of Canterbury and the then editor of *The Times* no less, William Rees Mogg; some tried to ban *Good Vibrations* by the nice Beach Boys for – vibrating? We culled Manfred Mann's *Pretty Flamingo* because in the US a flamingo was a name for a prostitute, and until 1971, women were not allowed to go into Wimpy Bars on their own, after midnight – why? Because any woman out on their own at such an hour was a prostitute, of course. On the positive side, increasing availability of the contraceptive pill apart, the death penalty was abolished in 1965, and in 1967, laws criminalising abortion and male homosexuality were repealed – although the age of consent for homosexual men was set at twenty-one, against the heterosexual age of consent, which was sixteen.

So the 1970s were the old 1960s in some ways: it was in the 1970s that we threw off many, but by no means all, of the 'old school' establishment ways and started to live something like a liberal life, and that included women and 'foreigners' as well. Unfortunately, all this new-found freedom coincided with a wave of terrorist outrages, a wave of outrageous industrial (non-)relations and an over-hasty waving goodbye to our industrial foundation and heritage, and to lots of jobs.

The Dire Economic Situation

Oil crisis, three-day week, sick man of Europe, Social Contract, Winter of Discontent are all phrases that define the 1970s and which continue to haunt us and still resonate today. 1970s Britain is characterised as a decade of relative economic decline, afflicted by inflation and strikes as both the Conservative government of 1970–74 under Edward Heath and the Labour government led by Harold Wilson and from 1976 James Callaghan were at a loss as to how to reverse the economic malaise. For the record, unemployment was still low at 3 per cent nationally in 1970 when Heath came to power.

But by 1972, unemployment passed the 1 million mark, peaking at over 1.5 million in 1978. Things were exacerbated in 1973 with the oil crisis that led to the three-day week in 1973–74. This, 'the first oil shock', was triggered when the members of the Organization of Arab Petroleum Exporting Countries (OAPEC, consisting of the Arab members of the OPEC plus Egypt and Syria) announced an oil embargo as a response to American involvement in the 1973 Yom Kippur War. By the end of the embargo in March 1974, the price of oil had rocketed from $3 per barrel to nearly $12 globally, with US prices much higher. A damaging series of strikes by coal miners and railway workers over the winter of 1973/74 added to the turmoil: Heath appealed to us to heat only one room in our houses; the UK, Germany, Italy, Switzerland and Norway banned flying, driving and boating on Sundays. Sweden rationed petrol and heating oil. The Netherlands imposed prison sentences on anyone who exceeded their ration of electricity.

Interestingly, much of the resulting massive windfall in oil revenues went on arms purchases that served to raise the political temperature and increase tensions in the Middle East. Saudi Arabia spent over $100 billion over the next few decades to spread its fundamentalist interpretation of Islam, Wahhabism, all over the world through religious charities such as al-Haramain Foundation, which bankrolled Sunni extremist groups such as Al-Qaeda and the Taliban. The consequences of this are still afflicting us today.

Harold Wilson's Social Contract was an attempt to head off the fractious industrial relations between government and unions. In return for the repeal of the 1971 Industrial Relations Act, food subsidies and a freeze on rent increases, the TUC would persuade its members to cooperate in a programme of voluntary wage restraint.

The toxic combination of destructive industrial strife with ballooning inflation and unemployment earned Britain the nickname the 'sick man of Europe', a term originally smeared on Turkey in the nineteenth century. By 1978, some 1.5 million people were unemployed, nearly three times the figure of a decade earlier, giving a national rate of over 5 per cent. It had not fallen below 1 million since 1975 and has persisted above this level ever since.

In the winter of 1978/79, we endured another series of public sector strikes – the Winter of Discontent, which put an end to Callaghan's Labour government in March 1979. Margaret Thatcher came to power and introduced new economic policies, including privatisation and deregulation, reform of industrial relations and tax changes.

On the plus side, oil was discovered in the North Sea, off Scotland. But many silver linings in 1970s Britain seem to have been accompanied by its own cloud: unfortunately, our oil's contribution to the UK economy was in part offset by the need to pay back an escalating national debt, and for welfare payments to the growing number of unemployed.

Many coal mines closed over the decade as the demand for coal in Britain declined – electricity was now generated by power stations burning oil or gas from the North Sea or by the use of nuclear energy. This was to have enormous social implications and an impact on industrial relations. The mood in the country was ugly, whichever side of the political fence you sat on:

> When England was a kingdom, we had a king. When we were an empire, we had an emperor. Now we're a country … and we have Margaret Thatcher.
>
> Kenny Everett, live on BBC Radio in 1981

The £ in Your Pocket

In 1971, Britain went decimal. Before this there was 12*d* (pennies) in a shilling and 20*s* (shillings) in a pound. A guinea was £1 and 1*s*. There were sixpences (tanners) for you to choke on at Christmas, and iconic three-penny bits, half-crowns, florins and halfpennies.

Domestic Goods

Sixty-four per cent of homes now had a washing machine. In 1974, the first domestic microwave cooker was sold amid fears of radioactive baked beans and purple-glowing porridge. In 1978, the VHS video recorder went on sale – although now largely defunct, many of its controls remain a mystery to this day. The year 1979 saw Sony begin selling the Walkman personal stereo – the beginning of the end of the days when people talked and listened to each other. We could, of course, now watch television programmes in magnificent colour with no fewer than three stations broadcasting in colour from 1967 to 1969. In 1971, 91 per cent of families had a TV, somewhat fewer a TV licence. The year 1972 saw the launch of John Craven's *Newsround*, recognition at last that children and teenagers were an important TV audience and that *Andy Pandy* was simply not good enough.

1970s Inventions – Whatever Did We Do Before?

1971 Digital watch – George Theiss / Willy Crabtree
1971 E-mail – Ray Tomlinson

1971 Pocket calculator – Sharp
1971 Personal computer – MITS
1972 The word processor
1975 Digital camera – Steven Sasson / Kodak
1979 Post-it notes – Spencer Silver / 3M
1979 Mobile phone – NTT
1979 Walkman – Akio Morita

Toys and Games

Barbie, Sindy and Action Man dolls took over the world. Action Man's distinctive facial scar has its own trademark protection.
1970 The Stylophone
1971 The Space Hopper
1973 The Chopper bike
1975 Pong: Atari's electronic table tennis game
1976 Stunt Kites
1977 Skateboards
1978 *Star Wars* merchandise
1979 Trivial Pursuit
Also popular were Spirograph, a game designed by mathematician Bruno Abakanowicz in the late nineteenth century to measure the area of a space defined by curves, and Play-Doh, developed in the 1930s as a product that could clean coal residue from wallpaper.

1970s Fashion

We use the term advisedly. Platform shoes, flared trousers and loons were all the rage. Hot pants were popular with some girls and women, while the midi dress and the maxi dress gradually took over from shorter hems. David Bowie, Elton John, Sweet, Slade and T. Rex led the charge towards glam and glitter. Their music was good too. Among boys and men, long hair was *de riguer* and getting longer. But the punks changed all that with some spectacular hairdos.

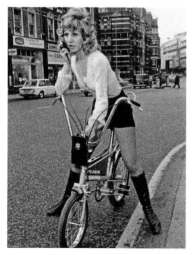

The radiotelephone chopper bike in March 1971, as demonstrated at the Ideal Home Exhibition at Olympia.

Transport

Global travel took off in 1970 when the first Pan Am Boeing 747 jet landed at Heathrow. After years of trialling and testing, Anglo-French *Concorde* – the fastest passenger aeroplane in the world – entered service in 1976. It could fly you to Bahrain or New York at around 2,100 kph. Popular cars were the Triumph TR7, two-door Capri and the MGB GT in 1978.

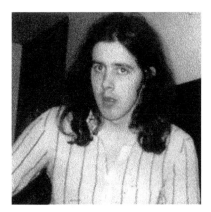

The author in 1975 at Hull University.

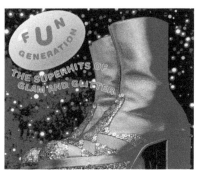

An album cover for a 1970s glam compilation.

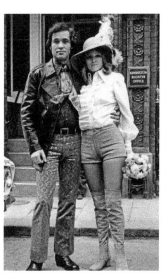

The height of 1970s fashion.

2

1970s York

York Celebrations Choir

The choir was formed in the late 1960s out of a desire to amalgamate York's many good small- and medium-sized choirs to create 'a choir of large forces which would be able to undertake major choral works'. The plan was to give York a choir of around 400 voices: after a series of meetings, Celebrations Choir was created, and the first concert was given in York Minster on 7 November 1970 before 1,500 people. The choir was poised to participate as a major force in the 1971 Celebrations year.

As well as numerous concerts, an association was formed with Yorkshire Television's *Stars on Sunday* programme with nine performances leading to recordings, which were screened almost weekly over several years. Three LPs were released: *A Choral Celebration in Honour of the 1900th Anniversary of the Founding of York, A Choral Festival – York Celebrations Choir* and *Great Sacred and Operatic Choruses*.

This list of events in 1971 gives a good idea of the choir's activities until its unfortunate demise in 1976.

June 4: York Records releases choir's first LP.

June 12: Verdi: *Requiem*, York Minster, with Royal Philharmonic Orchestra.

June 13: Verdi: *Requiem*, Royal Festival Hall, London.

June 27: Recording at Yorkshire Television, Kirkstall Road, Leeds, for *Stars on Sunday*.

July 4: Recording at Yorkshire Television, Kirkstall Road, Leeds, for *Stars on Sunday*, with Grimethorpe Colliery Band.

September 30: Concert, York Minster, with BBC Northern Symphony Orchestra. Walton: *Gloria*, Beethoven: *Choral Fantasia*; Gabrielli: *Sonata*; Janacek: *Sinfonietta*; Mozart: *Haffner Symphony*.

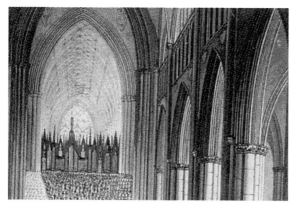

York Celebrations Choir by Alfred Gill (1898–1961, watercolour 1973), originally published in *York Minster Revealed* by York Civic Trust.

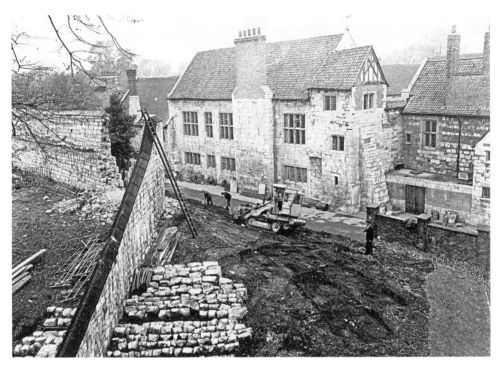

Above: Restoring the walls in 1970.

Below left: St George's Hall cinema being demolished in Castlegate next to Fairfax House.

Below right: Renovating shops in Shambles, April 1970.

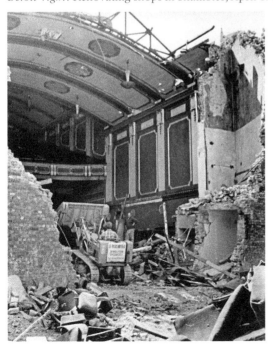

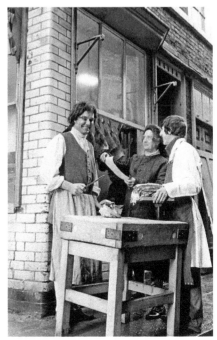

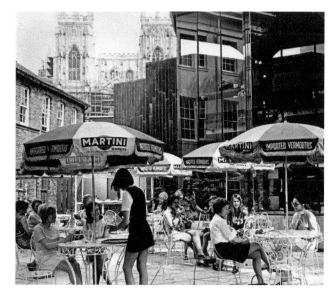

A touch of Paris comes to York outside the Theatre Royal.

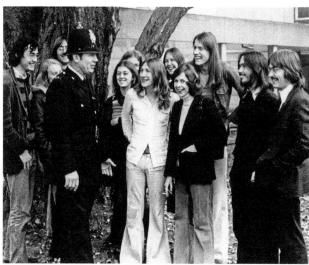

A policeman tries to buy a ticket for the Ian Dury concert at York University. (Photo courtesy of York University)

York University in the 1970s

Central Hall was the venue for the Who, The Kinks, Fairport Convention, John Martyn, Ian Dury and the Blockheads, Hot Chocolate, Humphrey Littleton, Acker Bilk, Paul Tortelier, Julian Bream, John Williams and others. Paul McCartney and Linda appeared one day out of the blue with their new band 'Wings' and performed a concert in Goodricke College Dining Room. Then they went to Hull.

Clubs and societies thrived, including the Winnie the Pooh Society, and the 'Turf Club', which met as an excuse to go to the races. And despite the fact that sports facilities consisted of just two playing fields, two squash courts and the sports hall, the annual 'Roses' event with Lancaster attracted hundreds of spectators.

Up to 600 students competed at the inter-college sports day. The drama society was prolific and at a festival in June 1972 produced six plays in one month: *Much Ado About*

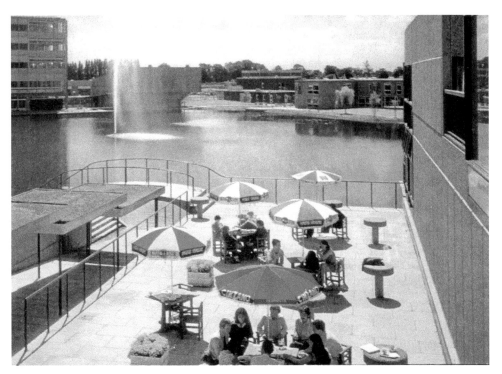

Life's a beach: York University life in the 1970s; it looks a lot tougher nowadays. (Photo courtesy of York University)

Nothing, Shakespeare's Farewell, Euripides' *The Bacchae, Uncle Vanya, Rosencrantz and Gildenstern* and *Private Lives.*

In 1973, the university provided a computerised results service for the RAC Rally. 'It placed a fast printing terminal and a VDU in the Rally Headquarters at the Royal Station Hotel. Results were sent to the Rally HQ via PO lines and then to the Rally control points to give both competitors and spectators the latest news of the event.'

Margaret Clitherow Made a Saint

The Margaret Clitherow Oratory in Shambles celebrates the life of Margaret Clitherow, who in 1970 became a saint. *Mulier fortis* – brave woman – she was the wife of John Clitherow, a butcher who lived here at No. 35 (or possibly at No. 10). They were married in St Martin-le-Grand in Coney Street. The house became a refuge for priests on the run. Margaret first saw the inside of a jail in 1577 (now the Castle Prison) for nine months for not attending church. She was jailed twice more at York Castle (1580 for six months and 1583 for eighteen months). Between 1582 and 1583, five priests were executed at Tyburn, and Margaret would go at night to the gallows to conduct a vigil over the bodies. She was found guilty in 1586 of 'harbouring and maintaining Jesuits and seminary priests, traitors to Her Majesty'. She had been betrayed by a Flemish boy in her care who had been threatened with a naked beating if he did not reveal the priest holes. The usual penalty for Margaret's transgression was hanging, but, because she refused to offer a plea ('having made no offence, I need no trial'), Margaret was sentenced to death by having a door weighted with nearly half a ton of boulders placed on top of her.

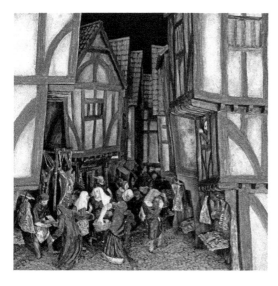

Life in Medieval York that would have been familiar to Margaret Clitherow. As shown in the 1970s *York Story*.

The execution took place at the tollbooth on the Ouse Bridge; within fifteen minutes she was dead – her ribcage had collapsed and burst through her skin. Her body was dumped but found later, apparently with no signs of decay. Margaret was beatified in 1929 and canonised in 1970 by Pope Paul VI, who described her as the 'Pearl of York'. Her embalmed hand is in the Bar Convent. A church in nearby Haxby is dedicated to her.

Haxby Wars

Between 1961 and 1971, the population of rural Haxby increased by over 50 per cent. In 1961, it was 2,407, in 1971 it stood at 3,783 and in 1981 it rose 240 per cent to 9,064 (in 1901 it was 711). Amenities to cater for this explosion in residents were something of an afterthought, as usual. Shops were one such amenity, and in 1970 they manifested themselves in a bleak-looking shopping centre, replacing Abel's farm and Bell's garage. Many residents were (and some still are) displeased by what was seen as an eyesore, completely out of step with the red-brick buildings and red roofs then characteristic of the village. This led, in 1976, to a conservation order restricting future developments to two storeys wherever possible, made of red-brick and red-clay pantiles. The incongruous Ashgrove complex next to the execrable shopping centre demonstrates how such orders can easily be ignored.

In 1978, a row erupted over Poor Folk's Close when a new housing development was proposed. Despite the fact that since 1733 the close had been a source of revenue to relieve poverty in the parish (hence the name, of course), the venal builders (devoid of any sense of history) objected that the name was not helping sales of their £16,000 bungalows. Astonishingly, Cherry Croft or Cherry Gardens were suggested as (more commercial) alternatives in line with the ubiquitous 'leafy suburb' names found in any and every leafy suburb. A compromise was eventually reached with Folk's Close, but another element of the village's heritage was thereby torpedoed.

Haxby's history does live on in some highly descriptive and meaningful road, school and street names: Calf Close, Eastfield Avenue, Hunter's Close, West Nooks, Dike Ray Close, Nether Windings, Golands Cottages and Headlands School are good examples. That said, we have lost some delightfully vivid names: Pudding Park, Pippins Pools, Hornett Nest

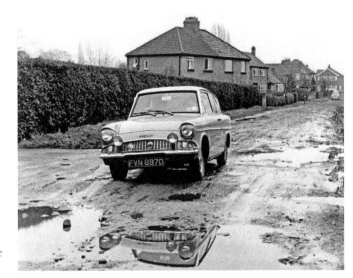

A Ford Anglia negotiating the potholes of The Avenue in 1972.

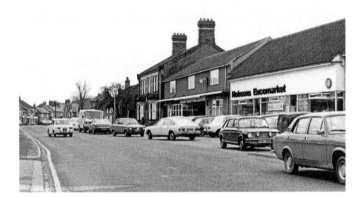

The Shopping Centre in The Village.

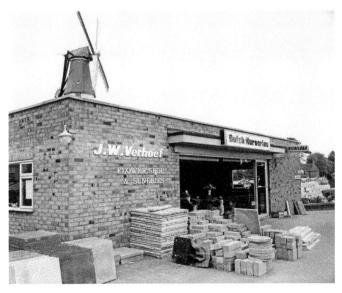

Dutch Nurseries in 1997.

Close, Beet Cottage (now The Cottage pub), Canary Bird Close, Lady Kell Lane (now the imaginatively named York Road, but happily revived in a development off Calf Close), to name but a few. The council plumbed new depths of dumbness and vanity when it recently named a new development, Reid Park, off Usher Lane, after one of their own.

York Theatre Royal in 1970

This list, and the ones that follow in subsequent years, gives just a few of the productions put on at the theatre this year and amply demonstrates the rich variety on offer:

Henry IV, Part 1	William Shakespeare
Sadler's Wells Opera	
Carmen (YAODS)	
Murder at the Vicarage	Agatha Christie
The Scarlet Pimpernel	Baroness Orczy
Narrow Road to the Deep North	Edward Bond
The Good Soldier Schweik	Jaroslav Hasek
Not Now Darling	Ray Cooney & John Chapman
Plaza Suite	Neil Simon
A Midsummer Night's Dream	William Shakespeare

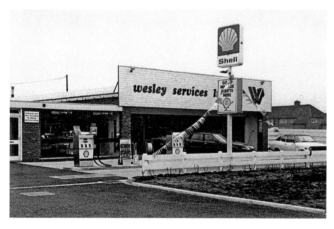

Wesley Services Garage in Station Road in 1977, now Pulleyn's.

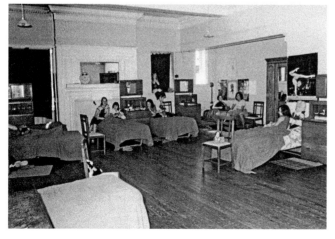

An early 1970s bedroom at the Mount School. Note the Olga Korbut poster on the wall and the pre-duvet bedspreads. Olga Valentinovna Korbut, the 'Sparrow from Minsk', is a former Belarusian gymnast who won four gold medals and two silver medals at the Olympic Games in 1972 and 1976 for the Soviet team.

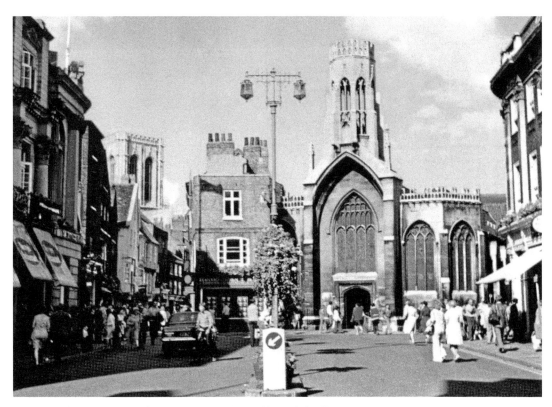

St Helen's Square in the 1970s – note the traffic and the flares.

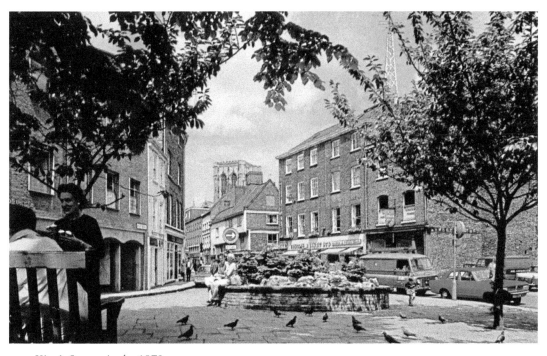

King's Square in the 1970s.

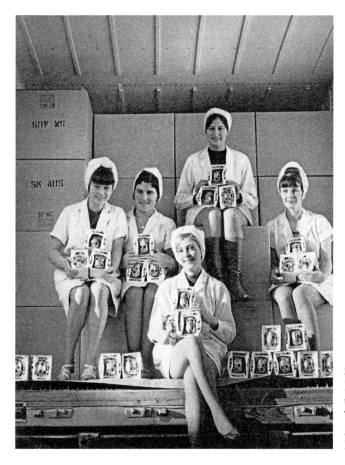

Some of the 75,000 Rowntree Easter eggs sent to Australia early in 1970. These girls posing for the *Evening Press* are from Rowntree's Card Box.

York Civic Trust Silver Jubilee

The year 1970 saw the Silver Jubilee of the foundation of York Civic Trust, responsible over the years for much priceless conservation and preservation work. To mark the occasion, a fountain was built in Exhibition Square – appropriately enough, close to the statue of city walls saviour William Etty. At the same time, it rid the city of an ugly car park.

The Trust said that year, 'We may have lost the All Gold of Terry's, but had in place acquired the Black Magic of Rowntree Mackintosh.'

The go-ahead was given for the refurbishment of redundant St Mary's Church in Castlegate to provide a permanent yet ever-changing exhibition of the city of York. The essentially medieval character of the church was retained; it was to become home to *York Story* in 1975, the council having bought the church for 5p.

3

YORK IN 1971

The 1,900th Anniversary of the Foundation of Eboracum

The Queen and the Duke of Edinburgh came to York on 28 June 1971 to celebrate the 1,900th anniversary of the founding of York by the Romans in AD 71. Proceedings that day began at Rufforth, where the Queen and the Duke left their aeroplane to be greeted by the Lord Lieutenant of York and the West Riding, Brigadier Kenneth Harding.

A Rolls-Royce flying the Royal Standard then swept them to Knavesmire where a twenty-one-gun salute boomed out to greet the Royal couple. A royal fly past comprising twenty-one Jet Provost aircraft from RAF Linton and RAF Leeming formed the letters ER in the sky soon after York's ancient Sword of State had been surrendered to the Queen by the Lord Mayor Alderman, Richard Scruton.

In the city, things started with a fanfare from regal trumpeters up on Micklegate Bar, heralding the entry of the Queen and Prince Philip into York, just like so many royal personages before them throughout the centuries. Traditionally, the royal party must ask the permission of the Lord Mayor to enter the city here. To date, no Lord Mayor has had the temerity to turn down a monarch. Crowds crammed the pavements on either side of Blossom Street six deep as the royal couple approached the bar in an open sovereign carriage, escorted by a troop of sixty Household Cavalry. Next day, the *Yorkshire Evening Press* proclaimed it a 'Triumphal Ride: colourful spectacle thrills thousands'. The cavalcade headed to the Assembly Rooms, where the Queen lunched with 250 guests.

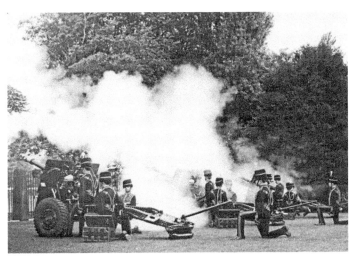

The twenty-one-gun salute at Knavesmire on 8 August marking the birthday of the Queen Mother.

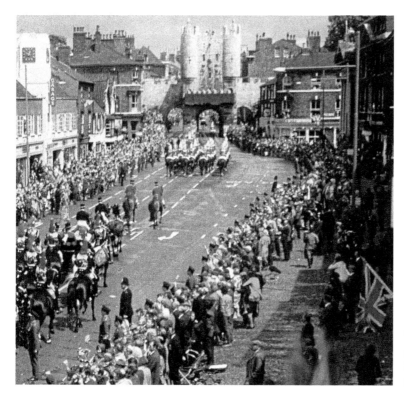

The Queen
approaches
Micklegate Bar
according to tradition.

This was the first time for more than 300 years that the Household Cavalry had ridden through the city.

Lunch at the Assembly Rooms included Scotch salmon and roast leg of lamb with asparagus. The royal couple watched a forty-five-minute excerpt from the *York Pageant,* which traced 1,900 years of the city's history since its founding by the Romans. They then joined 2,000 guests at a Garden Party in Museum Gardens.

If all appeared happy and well on the surface, then tensions and anxiety ran deep under the surface, as the report from *The Times* shows:

The visit by the Queen and the Duke of Edinburgh to York's 1,900th anniversary celebrations ended without incident this evening after a day of discreet but strict security precautions. A second letter threatening the Queen's life had been sent to the head office of the *Yorkshire Evening Press* in York. Like the first, it was printed in capitals and addressed to 'the Headitor'.

It read: 'The Angery Brigade wish to say that the Queen will be shot in the Museum Gardens. This is no fantasy.' The letter was posted in York on Sunday evening. It was handed to the police, who increased security along the royal route. More than 400 police officers were on duty ...

The Queen and the Duke of Edinburgh rode in an open carriage from York racecourse to the city centre a mile away. Four Army Scout cars, not in the original schedule, joined the procession, and York police said that uniformed and plain-clothes officers had been armed with pistols and rifles. These were not evident, although a detective was seen walking through York among the crowds with a rifle case slung over his shoulder.

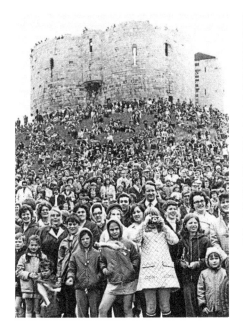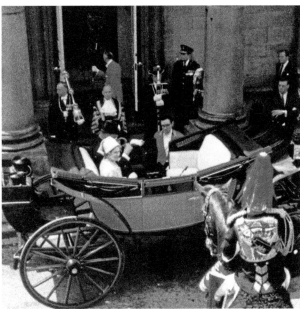

Above left: The crowds at the castle.

Above right: The Queen arriving at the Mansion House with reversed mace and sword.

In keeping with tradition, the mace and sword were duly reversed (as always in the presence of the monarch), and the city sword was surrendered to the Queen. But disaster struck when the Queen's coat became creased after a rain shower – a nearby dry-cleaner came to the rescue and pressed the coat in good time for the walkabout in the Museum Gardens.

The year of celebration began with a Roman-themed New Year's Eve ball in the Assembly Rooms, complete with Vestal Virgins and finished with the December production of Handel's *Messiah* in the Minster. In keeping with the sacred Roman tradition of keeping the Vestal flame alight at all times and at all costs, an eternal flame provided by the Gas Board blazed away in Library Square on top of a 12-foot-high column. Other events included the World Archery Championships, a Festival of Youth, the Pageant in the Museum Gardens in June and July celebrating nearly 2,000 years of York history and, at the Knavesmire, a medieval jousting tournament in which mounted knights in full armour jousted each other in the lists. In September, the Knavesmire played host to a quarter-scale model of a nuclear submarine for which thousands of people queued for a look at the submarine's replica control room. There was a six-day Services Searchlight Tattoo on Knavesmire also in September; £1 million worth of military hardware was on display, including a Thunderbird-guided missile, a Chieftain tank and a Navy Whirlwind helicopter. Five helicopters gave lunchtime aerial displays, including the aerial transportation of fuel in a giant net slung below the aircraft. There was replica of the pre-war Bootham Park galas with a spectacular fireworks finale, an Edwardian fair, a 1,900th celebration evening race meeting, the Sealed Knot procession and ball, and a re-enactment of the cremation of Emperor Severus after a torchlight procession. The Battle of Marston Moor was fought again.

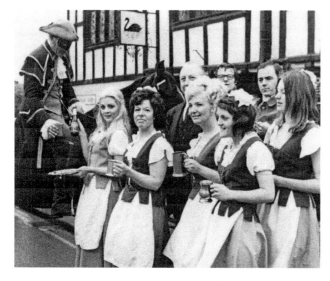

On 30 April 1971, Dick Turpin (Geoffrey Saville-Dean) shows up to sample a pint of Bass Charrington's Special Anniversary Ale outside the Black Swan.

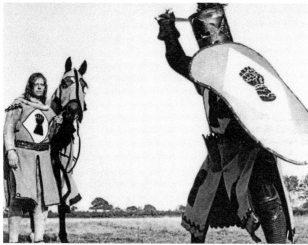

A rehearsal for the jousting tournament at the Knavesmire with Peter James as Senior Esquire and Max Diamond as Black Gauntlet on the right.

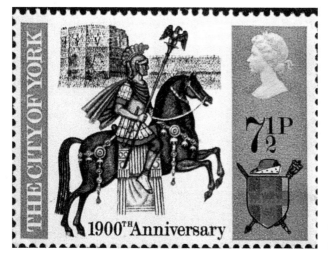

The commemorative postage stamp.

Commemorative stamps, medals, coins and goblets were produced. A special squad of guides was recruited – young women in blue uniforms who rode around on red scooters; they were based at the city's Information Bureau and called The Texaco Tourist Pilots.

What was the reason for this year-long extravaganza? York was founded twenty-eight years after the Roman invasion forces landed on the south coast during the reign of the Emperor Claudius in AD 43; from there they fanned out and headed east, west and north. The exact location of the landing is uncertain: it may have been Rutupiae (modern Richborough, in east Kent) or the Solent, landing at Bosham harbour near Noviomagus (Chichester) or at Southampton. Whatever, this was the third Roman invasion – the previous two were under the command of Julius Caesar in 44 and 43 BC and were cursory, exploratory affairs. Caesar's forays were followed by aborted plans for invasion under Augustus and the deranged Caligula. Claudius was looking for military glory and tribute; the natives too were restless with the pro-Roman Trinovantes displaced by the more aggressive Catuvellauni, who were putting anti-Roman pressure on neighbours, the Atrebates. Something had to be done about that and so it was that the Romans, under the command of Aulus Plautius, set sail from Bononia (modern Boulogne-sur-Mer) with four legions, amounting to around 20,000 men, plus 20,000 auxiliaries. The legions were Legio II Augusta, Legio IX Hispana, Legio XIV Gemina and Legio XX Valeria Victrix. Legio IX marched north and by AD 47 had established Lincoln (Lindum Colonia); the Romans were in control of an area south of a line from the Humber to the Severn Estuary. More success followed, notably in Wales where the troublesome Anglesey druids were massacred and where Caratacus was defeated in the Battle of Caer Caradoc; he fled to the Brigantes, a Roman client tribe based in the Pennines. But their queen, Cartimandua, turned him over to the Romans. Despite serious reverses during the Boudican Revolt in which Camulodunum (Colchester), Londinium (London) and St Albans were lost, the Romans continued their inexorable progress. Cartimandua sought Roman help when her husband Venutius rebelled. The governor, Quintus Petillius Cerialis, advanced from Lincoln to York, finally defeating Venutius near Stanwick around AD 70.

Eboracum, 'place of the yew trees', was occupied by the Romans from AD 71 until AD 410 when trouble in and around the empire elsewhere obliged them to leave Britannia for good. Cerialis and his IXth Legion built a military fortress (*castra*) here

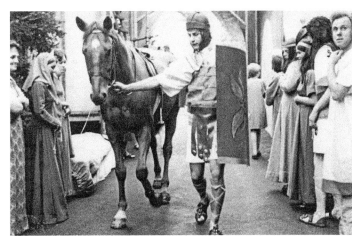

Roman soldier Graham Hollingsworth leads out his horse on the opening night of the pageant in Museum Gardens in June 1971 for the 1,900th York Pageant.

on the flat ground between the rivers Ouse and Foss. As with military settlements all over the empire, Eboracum acted as a magnet to civilians looking for commercial opportunities and a place from which to trade. By the end of the second century, the fortress was complemented by a network of streets, public and business buildings and private houses.

Strategically, York was of considerable military importance and a major communications centre. The original wooden camp was rebuilt by Agricola in AD 81 and completely rebuilt in stone in AD 108. Over 48,000 m^3 of magnesian limestone was used from the quarries at Calcaria (Tadcaster). The Colonia extended over 60 acres; the walls were 20 feet high and 4 feet thick in parts. The *Praetorium* (general's headquarters) is under the Minster. There is an amphitheatre and temple under Micklegate and a *forum basilica*, baths on the banks of the Ouse, and a sewerage system in Bishophill. A VIth Victrix Legion column stands proud opposite the Minster. Parts of the limestone walls survive, as does the ten-sided Multangular Tower in Museum Gardens; the lower 20 feet are Roman, dating from around 310 and constitute the only such surviving tower in Britain. It formed the western extremity of the fortress and features a stone wall 21 feet high by 11 feet wide, bearing the legible inscription '*Genio loci feliciter*' – 'good luck to the guardian spirit of this place'. Its name originates in 1683, before that it was called Ellerendyng or Elrondyng. Another Multangular Tower apparently stood in Feasegate.

Hadrian visited in AD 122 en route to plan his wall, replacing the IXth with the VIth legion. Septimius Severus, Rome's first black emperor, lived in York between AD 208 and AD 211; his sons, Caracalla and Geta, were declared co-emperors in AD 198 and 209. Severus died in York in 211 and received a spectacular funeral in the city, but not before he had declared York to be the capital of Britannia Inferior. According to Cassius Dio, the Roman biographer, the emperor uttered these final words to his sons: 'Don't argue with each other, make the soldiers rich, and ignore everyone else.' Severus was cremated outside the fortress wall. Dio again:

> His body arrayed in military garb was placed upon a pyre, and as a mark of honour the soldiers and his sons ran about it and as for the soldier's gifts, those who had things at hand to offer them put them upon it and his sons applied the fire.

By AD 237, Eboracum had been elevated to the status of a *colonia*, the highest legal status a Roman city could achieve – it was one of only four in Britain. Around the same time, Eboracum became self-governing, with a council made up of rich merchants and resettled veteran soldiers.

A statue of Constantine near the Minster celebrates his proclamation as emperor here in AD 306 on the death in York of his father, the Emperor Constantius Chlorus. It also pays tribute to his conversion to Christianity, probably in AD 312 when, for the first time, it was not illegal, and dangerous, to be a Christian in the Roman Empire.

In the eighteenth and nineteenth centuries, interest in Roman York proliferated. Many distinguished York residents such as Martin Lister (1638–1712), an eminent zoologist, delivered papers on, for example, the Bishophill altar to the Philosophical Transactions of the Royal Society. He was the first scholar to identify the Multangular Tower as a Roman structure. Francis Drake (1696–1771), a local surgeon, published his Eboracum in 1736 basing much of it on Lister's work but peppering it with speculation and legend, leading him to claim that the emperor Constantine was born in York and that Helena, his mother, was British.

William Hargrove, a local newspaper proprietor and journalist, prefixed his *History of York*, published in 1818, as follows, in what must be one of the earlier salvoes in the ongoing battle of the north–south divide:

> In the earliest records of English History, Ebor, Eboracum or York, is represented as a place of great importance; and, in the zenith of meridian splendour, it was the residence of Imperial Power, and the legislative seat of the Roman Empire. Hence we may readily suppose, especially when the ancient historic accounts of this city are contrasted with those of London, that York far exceeded in dignity and consequence, if not in population and extent, the present capital of the British Empire, at that period.

Hargrove published new material on the Mithraic relief found in 1747 near St Martin-cum-Gregory Church and the inscription from a temple of Serapis found on Toft Green in 1770. The mantle was then taken up by the Revd Charles Wellbeloved (1769–1858), one of the founders of the Yorkshire Philosophical Society in 1822 and the first honorary curator of antiquities in the society's museum, now the Yorkshire Museum. In 1842, he published his Eboracum, covering the discovery of the fortress defences destroyed during the creation of St Leonard's Place and Exhibition Square in 1835 – the extent of the legionary fortress and remains of a great baths complex, some remains of which were revealed during the building of the first railway station in 1839–40.

In the late 1960s and early 1970s, the Royal Commission on Historical Monuments for England carried out excavations at the Minster while the central tower was being shored up. This was the very heart of the legionary fortress, but the primary aim was to locate the Anglo-Saxon Minster referred to by the venerable Bede as the site of King Edwin of Northumbria's baptism in AD 627. This, however, proved elusive, and it was decided to focus on things Roman: the walls of the headquarters, basilica and barracks were discovered dating from the first to the fifth centuries. Work began re-excavating a late Roman stone tower built into the Roman fortress wall near the Multangular Tower. This was first discovered in 1842 and is now known misleadingly as the 'Anglian Tower'; York City Council put the tower on permanent display and, as part of the 1971 celebrations, exposed an adjacent stretch of the fortress wall by removing the overlying medieval rampart.

The needs of 5,000 troops created a vibrant economy and some important light industry: military tile kilns have been excavated in the Aldwark–Peasholme Green area, glass-working at Coppergate, metal-works and leather-works producing military equipment in Tanner Row. Eboracum was also the major manufacturing centre for Whitby Jet (*gagates* in Latin), used from the early third century in jewellery and exported throughout Britain and into Europe. There are fewer than twenty-five surviving jet pendants from Roman times, of which six are from Eboracum and now in the Yorkshire Museum.

The Roman bathhouse excavated under the Roman Bath pub (formerly The Mail Coach, The Barrel Churn, The Cooper and The Barrel) in 1930 is partly visible, including cold room (*frigidarium*), hot room (*caldarium*) and under-floor central heating system (*hypocaust*). Tiles stamped *Legio VI* and *Legio IX* have been uncovered, confirming that legions were stationed at Eboracum.

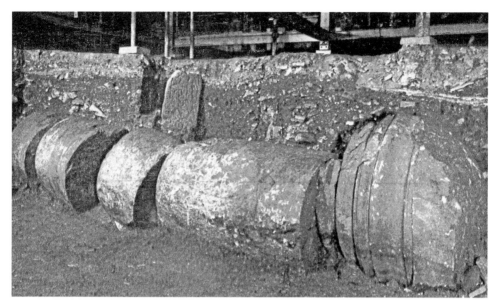

The column when it was found in 1968.

Roman Column Re-erected

In 1971, York Civic Trust re-erected a Roman column. A fine 9.5-m-high column from the Great Hall, or *principia*, was discovered beneath the south transept of the Minster during excavations in 1969; it was re-erected outside the south door of the Minster in 1971 to commemorate the city's 1,900th birthday. Thirty-five more columns are awaiting excavation. This one was found lying on its side in pieces. The *principia* may well have been the building in which Constantine was declared emperor in AD 306. Lord (Kenneth) Clark of *Civilisation* fame did the honours at the unveiling.

The quotation on the plaque reads,

> THIS ROMAN COLUMN ONCE STOOD WITHIN THE GREAT HALL OF THE HEADQUARTERS BUILDING OF THE FORTRESS OF THE SIXTH LEGION (WHOSE EMBLEM WAS A BULL) IN THE FOURTH CENTURY A.D. IT WAS FOUND IN 1969 DURING THE EXCAVATION OF THE SOUTH TRANSEPT OF THE MINSTER, LYING WHERE IT HAD COLLAPSED. IT WAS GIVEN BY THE DEAN AND CHAPTER TO THE YORK CIVIC TRUST WHO IN 1971 ERECTED IT ON THIS SITE TO MARK THE 1900TH ANNIVERSARY OF THE FOUNDATION OF THE CITY BY THE ROMANS IN A.D. 71.

York Chamber Pot comes to Light

12 November 1971 was the day when the most bizarre of discoveries was dug up in York: a fifteenth-century gentleman's chamber pot was found by workmen excavating foundations for York's telephone extension. The pot, measuring around 8 inches in diameter with a 3-inch-wide opening and handle was said to be the first item of its kind that Allen Butterwood, then curator of the city museum, had ever seen.

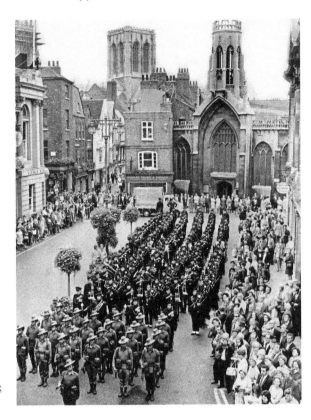

15 September saw 160 Gurkha bandsmen marching through York; here they are in St Helen's Square.

'He had no doubt that this was a piece of gentleman's apparatus – kept out of sight in a 15th-century bed chamber – and should go on show, but was unable to provide a suitable name for it,' read a report in the then *Yorkshire Evening Press*.

Welcome Back George Hudson – All is Forgiven

When George Hudson was disgraced in 1849, the authorities in York could not move quickly enough to rename George Hudson Street – imaginatively, they settled on Railway Street. It was as if to extinguish all memory of Hudson – a kind of *damnatio memoriae*. But in 1971, one hundred years after his death, the authorities in York had second thoughts and the original name was restored to the street. George Hudson was born again!

'The Railway King', George Hudson, was a prime mover in York's development as a major railway city; his advice to George Stephenson was to make York, his adopted city, a hub: *'Mak all t'railways cum t'York'*. Stephenson took that advice, and with the railway tracks came a significant boost to local industry and tourism; the visitors flocked in and still flock in to this day.

Hudson also deserves credit for his part in establishing the arterial line from King's Cross to Edinburgh Waverley, although his reputation will always be stained with illegal financial malpractice, chicanery and a distinct lack of transparency in his commercial and political dealings.

For Hudson, 1821 was a big year: he gained a share in the business he worked in and married the owner's daughter, Elizabeth; they had seven children together. When Bell retired, the firm became Nicholson & Hudson, and by 1827, the company was

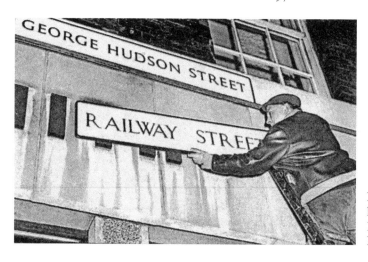

Now you don't see him, now you do. Rehabilitating George Hudson.

the largest business in York. In 1827, he had the good fortune to be left £30,000 by his great-uncle, Matthew Botrill. Hudson had been rather over solicitous in caring for Botrill during his illness, a fact that has raised suspicions regarding the legality of the bequest. He used the money to inveigle and buy himself into the York establishment. The Hudsons moved from College Street to a house in the more salubrious Monkgate.

Hudson converted from being a Methodist and a Dissenter to a High Church Tory, becoming treasurer of the York Conservative Party in 1832. He had a prominent role in the establishment of the York Union Banking Co. with Glyn's as their London agent. In 1835, he was elected to York City Council and became alderman in 1837 and Lord Mayor for 1837/38. This event was marked by an extravagant banquet in honour of the Archbishop of York followed by a ball to honour the York Hussars.

In 1833, Hudson set off on his long roller-coaster journey on the railways of England. He attended a meeting at what was then Tomlinson's Hotel in Low Petergate to discuss the construction of the railway line from York to connect with the Leeds to Selby line. Perceptively, he bought 500 shares, making him the largest shareholder. It was at this time that he had the pivotal discussion with George Stephenson to route the London–Newcastle line through York rather than Leeds.

The required Act of Parliament was passed in 1837, eased through with the help of £3,000 in Hudson bribes – this may not have been that difficult to fix as at the time there were 155 MPs in the House who were directors of railway companies. Hudson became chairman of the new company, to be known as the York & North Midland Railway Co. (YNMR), with George Stephenson as the engineer. He then raised £5,000,000 to link the Midlands with Scotland persuading people to invest by guaranteeing a 6 per cent dividend. Work started on the YNMR line in April 1837, complete with a new station inside the walls in York. The opening of the junction on the Leeds to Selby line took place on 29 May 1839 and at Normanton on 1 July 1840: London was now linked by rail to York. The YNMR leased the Leeds & Selby Railway for £17,000 per year: Hudson lost no time closing the line so that passengers had no choice but to travel on his tracks via Castleford.

With astonishing speed, a raft of other northern lines were opened or brought into Hudson's orbit around this time. In July 1844, Pickering and Scarborough was approved, and in June 1845, the Whitby & Pickering Railway was bought by the YNMR. York to Pickering opened in July 1845, affording a through-route from York to Whitby where Hudson owned property. York to Scarborough, which Hudson regarded as potentially the 'Brighton of the north', opened on that same day despite objections regarding the company accounts from Joseph Rowntree. On 1 July 1845, the YNMR took out a lease on the Hull & Selby Railway and in October became joint lessee of the Manchester, Sheffield & Lincoln Railway. In 1846, lines from Seamer to Filey and Hull to Bridlington were completed; the following year, the line between Filey and Bridlington opened. The YNMR line to Harrogate opened between Church Fenton and Spofforth, as did the line from York to Market Weighton. On 8 May 1848, Hull Paragon station opened and the line from Spofforth to Harrogate was completed. The Selby and Market Weighton link was opened with the line to Beverley following some years later. A direct line to Leeds was on the cards but abandoned after Hudson's demise in 1849. Visible evidence remains at the redundant railway viaduct at Tadcaster.

By 1847, Hudson companies now controlled 1,450 of the 5,000 miles of track in England; he was in charge of the Midland, the York and North Midland, the York, Newcastle and Berwick, and the Eastern Counties companies – he was indisputably the Railway King. It was revealed in 1845 that Hudson had £319,835 invested in railway shares. He purchased a controlling interest in the Newcastle & North Shields Railway and the Great North of England Railway. His kingdom now stretched from Bristol to Berwick.

Business and politics came in equal measure to George Hudson. In 1846, he shunted through thirty-two parliamentary bills for railway projects costing some £10 million. The same year, he emerged from the political sidings to achieve what he considered as the pinnacle of his life: he was elected Tory MP for Sunderland at the 1845 General Election, largely won on the promise to bail out the failing Monkwearmouth Dock and the Durham & Sunderland Railway. Hudson companies now controlled over 25 per cent of the railways in England. When Hudson became an MP, he bought a property in Albert Gate in Knightsbridge. Today it is home, no less, to the French embassy.

Meanwhile, on the surface, all seemed well with Hudson; in January 1846, *The Standard* newspaper published this eulogy:

> Two hundred thousand well paid labourers, representing as heads of families, nearly one million men, women and children, all feast through the bold enterprise of one man. Let us hear what man or class of man ever before did so much for the population of a country.

But *Punch* was on his case after a railway accident at Romford in 1846, allegedly due to savage cost cutting:

> by reason of the misconduct, negligence and insobriety of drivers and sundry stokers, engineers, policemen, and others, your Majesty's subjects, various and several collisions, explosions and oversettings are continually taking place on the railways, your Majesty's dominion.

Surreptitiously, George Hudson was making use of privileged information and insider dealing to manipulate share prices – profiting handsomely. In 1847, the financial irregularities that would eventually lead to Hudson's demise started to emerge. Hudson's railway bubble had burst. In 1848, a damning pamphlet entitled *The Bubble of the Age or The Fallacy of Railway Investment, Railway Accounts and Railway*

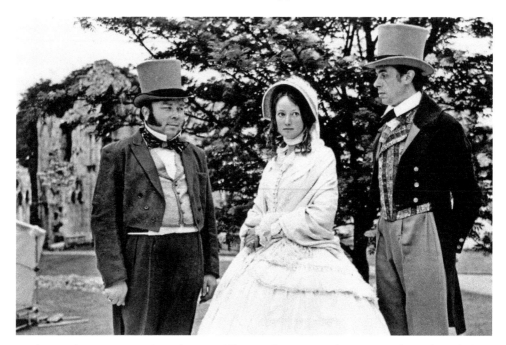

Hudson with Queen Victoria and Prince Albert in the 1971 York Pageant. The real royals here look apprehensive, although they cannot have guessed what was round the corner.

Dividends alleged that the dividend paid by Hudson's companies were paid out of capital rather than revenue.

Share prices tumbled and a long-awaited backlash began with undisguised relish. Many who had invested heavily in railway shares were ruined. Hudson had hit the buffers: he resigned from many of his company directorships and had to repay large sums of money, which had allegedly been misappropriated. In 1849, he was expelled from York City Council, and, ignominiously, his effigy at Madame Tussauds was reduced to a puddle of melted wax.

The Times summed up the ugly mood one morning in 1848:

> It was a system without rules, without order, without even a definite morality. Mr. Hudson, having a faculty for amalgamation, and being so successful, found himself in the enjoyment of a great railway despotism, in which he had to do everything out of his own head and among lesser problems to discover the ethics of railway speculation and management.

Despite agreeing to pay everything back, Hudson fled the country, and his creditors. He settled in Boulogne, audaciously returning to England in 1865 for his brother Charles' funeral, and to fight the seat at Whitby in the general election that year. However, before a vote was cast, Hudson was arrested by the Sheriff of York and imprisoned at York from July 1865 to October 1866. He was eventually released when the debt for which he was incarcerated was paid off by Tory MP Sir George Elliot, the Atlantic cable pioneer. Elliot and fellow MP Hugh Taylor set up a subscription fund, which they launched with a donation of 100 guineas each. It was converted into a trust fund, protected from Hudson's creditors, and provided Hudson with a yearly income of £600. He then moved to Pimlico in London with his wife to live quietly in virtual anonymity.

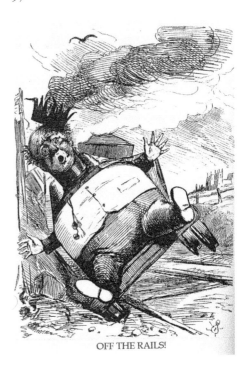

The joke's very much on Hudson now ...
Leech's cartoon in *Punch* in 1849.

OFF THE RAILS!

Hudson fell ill in York in December 1871; he returned to London where he died at home. Ironically, his coffin was taken by train back to York from where he was conveyed and buried at Scrayingham, near to his birthplace. Hudson's estate was worth less than £200.

Corruption notwithstanding, George Hudson had nevertheless established York as a major railway centre. His lasting legacy was the formation of the North Eastern Railway in 1854, headed by Hudson's enemy George Leeman. York to London could now be done in five hours. Ethical and principled Hudson was not, but he was a visionary and made an invaluable and unrivalled contribution to the railways of England. In 1849, in a lame attempt to erase him from local history, George Hudson Street in York was renamed Railway Street; in 1971, the street was renamed again after the Railway King who had presciently brought the railways to York. The old Adelphi pub on the corner of Micklegate took the name 'The Railway King', and a plaque decorates the walls of former homes at No. 44 Monkgate and No. 1 College Street. Ironically, and sadly, George Hudson Street shares with Leeman Road the distinction of being one of York's shabbiest streets. His name also lives on at Hudson House, formerly the 1968 offices for the North eastern region of British Rail.

It seems that York has always agonised over Hudson, finding it difficult to reconcile his arrant corruption with the priceless and lasting contribution he made to the city. In 1845, *The Yorkshire Gazette* neatly summed up the adulation in which he was held:

> Why is old York like New York? Because in both 'The Hudson' facilitates commercial communication, and has established power and wealth.

The York and County appealed for Hudson's rehabilitation in 1968 when it called 'Hudson come back, all is forgiven', echoed in the *1969–70 York Civic Trust Annual Report*:

There is no doubt that George Hudson brought to the City a lasting and important place in the life of the railways of this country ... we should make an end to his disgrace.

Memories, of course, are short, and the passage of time can act as a purging filter on the real facts. Vital as his legacy is, visionary that he was, the fact remains that Hudson was a charlatan and a cheat. However, his treatment over the years by the city of his birth is at best shabby, at worst, ignorant. His contribution to York is inestimable and while Guy Fawkes and Dick Turpin have achieved cult status, Hudson, like Joseph's Terry and Rowntree, those other huge York benefactors, remains visually obscure and something of a civic embarrassment. Where are the monuments to all three? Although he robbed many, Hudson neither killed, nor plotted to kill, anyone as did Fawkes and Turpin. Perhaps it is best to let *The Times* have the last word, in this extract from its obituary of Hudson on 16 December 1871:

> The first tide in his affairs led on to fortune, but he was afterwards stranded, and neither he nor his schemes could float. A quarter of a century ago he turned all he touched to gold; in after years his name was enough to wither the prospectus in which it was printed. The world which blindly trusted him, which cringed to him and flattered him, avenged itself by excessive and savage reprobation.

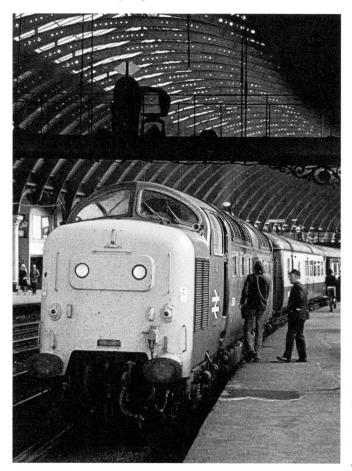

One of Hudson's numerous legacies: a Class 55 Deltic Co-Co No. 55016 *Gordon Highlander* forming the 14.00 Kings Cross to Edinburgh on 23 August 1977 at York station. (Photo J. H. Cooper-Smith)

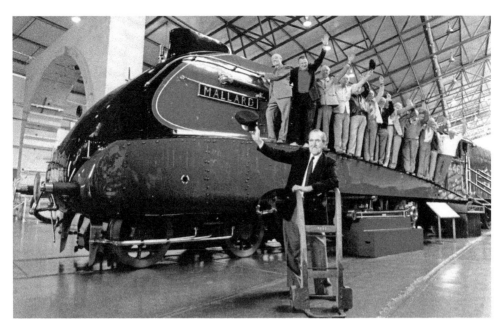

Another legacy: the truly iconic *Mallard* at the National Railway Museum in 1993. Fireman Jim Fletcher and former drivers had gathered to celebrate the 30th anniversary of its retirement in 1963.

Saluting Station

In 1971, York was made an army Saluting Station, firing gun salutes five times a year on events such as the queen's birthday. The date marked 1,900 years of army in York.

Population

1971 – Population of Britain was 54 million.
The population of York was as follows:

1961	144,585	+7.0 per cent
1971	154,749	+7.0 per cent
1981	158,170	+2.2 per cent

Fifty Years of the Rotary Club

The public clock mounted on the wall in Minster Gates carries this inscription:

> This clock was given to the City of York in its 1,900th year by the Rotary Club of York in its 50th year – 1971

It was the brainchild of that year's club president, Vincent Fisher; the £600 it cost was met by the donations of club members. The Lord Mayor, Councillor Vic Boulton, was invited 'to accept the clock as an acknowledgement by each Member of the Rotary Club of York of the happiness derived in fellowship and service and in the pride and privilege we feel in our citizenship of this great City'. In accepting the gift, the Lord Mayor described it as 'most sensible, most useful and a reminder of our ancient heritage'.

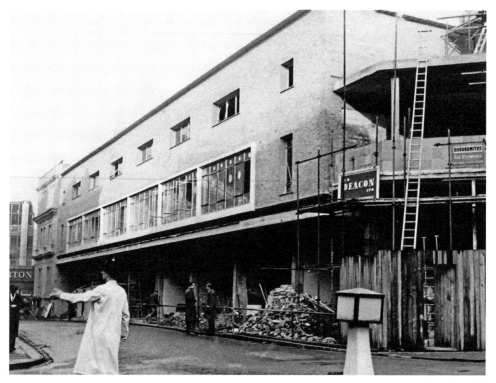

Spurriergate, January 1971. More shops going up.

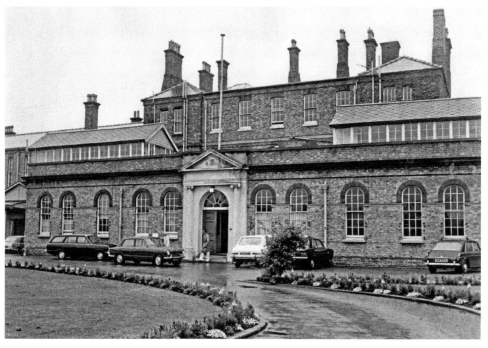

York Military Hospital, August 1971, scheduled to come down.

York Theatre Royal in 1971

Orpheus in the Underworld (YLOS)	Offenbach
Halfway Up the Tree	Peter Ustinov
The Royal Ballet Company	
Sadler's Wells Opera	
The Sound of Music (YAODS)	
Hadrian VII	Peter Luke
What the Butler Saw	Joe Orton
Fiddlers Five	Agatha Christie
Stringer's Last Stand	Stan Barstow & Alfred Bradley
Les Fourberies De Scapin	(Theatre de Bourgogne)
Great Expectations	Charles Dickens

The 500th Anniversary of the Cathedral and Metropolitical Church of St Peter in York

The year 1971 marked 500 years since the completion of the 300-year construction of York Minster, which was an important anniversary by any standard, but especially important for the city of York – to many York Minster is York; to many more still York is York Minster. On 1 July, more than 2,000 Friends of York Minster congregated to celebrate the 500th anniversary at a special service led by Dr Michael Ramsey, Archbishop of Canterbury.

The official name is The Cathedral and Metropolitical Church of St Peter in York. It was once thought to tower over a site of an earlier Norman cathedral that was almost as big; we now know that it is the Roman *principia* that lies underneath, not an earlier cathedral. The present Minster took 250 years to build from 1220 to 1471.

The five-year-long restoration of York Minster after the detailed and alarming inspections of 1965 and 1966 culminated in 1971, when the incipient collapse of the central tower and other calamitous cracks and structural defects were comprehensively arrested. It was the most important work to be done here since the fifteenth century; essentially, the central tower was found to be sinking. Speed was of the essence – not because the tower was about to come crashing down into the nave but because the fabric of the building was rapidly reaching a point (fifteen years hence at the outside) when it would be too weak to survive the stresses and strains of extensive repair work. An appeal for £2 million was launched. The central tower and the east and west gables were underpinned and stabilised with concrete and steel; the inside and outside of the building were cleaned. The ominous lean and bow of the Great East Window was also rectified.

While the central tower was being stabilised, archaeologists were working away, frantically but methodically uncovering layers of York's history from Roman times through to the late Middle Ages and beyond. Perhaps the most significant discovery was that the Norman church built by Thomas of Bayeux, thought for centuries to be under the present Minster, was, in fact, not there after all. Instead, they unearthed a Saxon and Viking burial ground and, most significantly, the Roman *principia*, or military headquarter building.

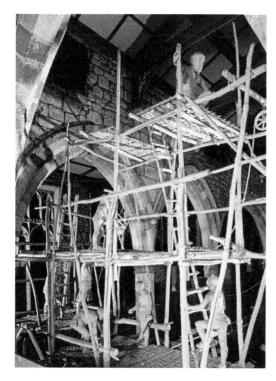

Medieval scaffolding, as shown in the 1970s *York Story*.

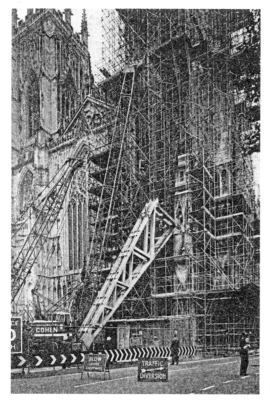

Scaffolding decorating the Minster.

What makes the Minster so splendid? Here are twenty-five reasons why it is truly awesome and truly iconic, to use modern parlance:

- It took 252 years to build the Minster, to make it more or less as it appears today.
- 60 per cent of all England's medieval stained glass resides in York Minster.
- The Minster contains 128 medieval windows.
- Each panel of glass in the Great East Window takes a conservator around 600 hours to fully restore. There are 311 panels in total.
- The 1408 Great East Window is the world's single largest medieval stained-glass window – the size of a tennis court.
- The Minster boasts 2 million pieces of glass.
- The Tower has a mechanised winch that hangs down from the central roof boss. This is used to suspend the Advent Wreath – probably the largest in the country – in December, and to hold a large wooden cross during Easter Week.
- York Minster's nativity service is the world's greatest unrehearsed nativity.
- The Central Tower is large enough to fit the Tower of Pisa inside.
- The Minster is one of only seven cathedrals in the world to have its own police force.
- The Central Tower collapsed in 1407 due to the soft soil beneath, and nearly collapsed again in the 1970s before major structural work reinforced its foundations. It weighs 16,000 tons.
- Edward I's parliament in 1297 was held in the Chapter House.
- 16 miles of scaffolding adorned the East End's 2015–16 exterior works.
- There are more than 5,000 possible changes in the Minster bells.
- There are 900,000 visitors to the Minster in a year.
- There are around 1,800 services held each year.
- It costs around £20,000 per day to keep the Minster running.
- There are 275 steps to climb before you get to the top.
- There have been ninety-seven archbishops of York since Paulinus in 627.
- There are seventeen altars.
- There have been ten major fires at the Minster.
- Kill Canon Corner is at the west front of the Minster – notorious for its powerful eddying winds. No clergy has died here to date.
- The length from the top of the choir screen is 157 ½ feet, breadth 46 ½ feet; there are sixty-four stalls.
- In January 2015, Libby Lane was ordained as the new Bishop of Stockport during a service at York Minster conducted by the Archbishop of York, Dr John Sentamu, and attended by nearly 2,000 people.

A York Minster Timeline

- AD 627 The first recorded church on the site was wooden, 'the Anglo-Saxon Cathedral', built in a hurry by Bishop Paulinus to provide a place in which to baptise King Edwin of Deira, on Easter Day that year.
- AD 630 Edwin then built something more substantial; his stone structure was completed in 637 by Oswald and dedicated to St Peter.

- AD 670 This church was dilapidated by 670 when St Wilfrid repaired and renewed the structure. The school and library were established, and by the eighth century it comprised some of the most substantial church buildings in Northern Europe.
- AD 741 The church was destroyed in a fire and rebuilt on a yet grander scale complete with thirty altars. Around AD 800, Alcuin describes the new church as 'lofty, splendid and graceful'. Waves of invaders came and went, plunging York into Dark Ages obscurity until the tenth century.
- AD 895 Danish King Guthfrith converted to Christianity and was buried in the Minster. Then there was a series of Benedictine archbishops, including St Oswal of Worcester, Wulfstan and Ealdred, who travelled to Westminster to crown William in 1066. Ealdred died in 1069 and was buried here.
- AD 1069 William's harrying of the North caused severe fire damage the church, but the first Norman archbishop, Thomas of Bayeux (r. 1070–1100), made invaluable repairs. The archbishop assembled canons and appointed a dean, treasurer and precentor, a chancellor, as well as various archdeacons and a number of clerks.
- AD 1075 The Danes wrecked the church, but it was rebuilt from 1080 in the Norman style; it was 111 m long. After another fire in 1137, the choir was extended and the crypt was rebuilt beginning from 1154 by Archbishop Roger of Pont L'Eveque; a large chapel dedicated to St Sepulchre was added to the nave. He also rebuilt the Archbishop's Palace.
- AD 1215 Archbishop Walter de Gray ordered the construction of a Gothic structure to rival Canterbury; building began in 1220.
- AD 1227 William Fitzherbert, Archbishop of York, was posthumously canonised and became St William of York. This encouraged pilgrims to visit York and boosted the Minster's tourist trade, competing with other shrines such as St John Lee's at Beverley Minster.
- AD 1250 The north and south transepts were the first to go up; both were in the Early English Gothic style. The substantial central tower was completed, with a wooden spire.
- AD 1260 The Chapter House was begun in the 1260s, completed before 1296.
- AD 1407 the central tower collapsed; the piers were then reinforced, and a new tower was built from 1420. The western towers were added between 1433 and 1472. The cathedral was declared complete and consecrated in 1472.
- The Minster suffered heavily during the English Reformation: the chantry chapels and altars were torn down in 1549 under Edward VI (r. 1547–53) and much of the cathedral plate was lost. In addition, St William's Shrine was destroyed: the Chantries and Chantry Priests were abolished, 'images' were removed, the seven daily services were reduced to three, and the English Liturgy and Clergy were introduced.
- Under Elizabeth I (r. 1558–1603), the interior of the Minster was stripped of its tombs, funereal brasses, memorials, altars, vestments, coats of arms and stained-glass portraits.
- AD 1632 Charles I donated £1,000 to be spent on redecorating the choir and on a new organ. In 1633, he stopped at the Minster en route to his coronation in Scotland, and complained about the shops springing up at the south façade between 1570 and 1586 – he had one removed.

- During the Civil War, York was besieged by parliamentary forces for eleven weeks; cannon shot smashed through some of the windows at the Minster. The roof was used to send fire signals to Royalist forces at Pontefract. When York surrendered after the Battle of Marston Moor, the Parliamentary forces held a service of thanksgiving in the Minster. The building was spared real damage due to the influence of Thomas Fairfax, Cromwell's general, who had a penchant for things antiquarian. A plan to dismantle the Chapter House came to nothing.
- AD 1644 Early plans for a university in York came to nothing. The idea was to use the Deanery, Bedern and prebendal houses.
- AD 1660 The restoration of the monarchy was mirrored by the restoration of the archbishop, dean and chapter.
- AD 1666 A signal turret was built onto the central tower.
- In 1730 Lord Burlington designed a new floor for the Minster in the neoclassical Palladian style. Installing the new marble floor involved the destruction of every tomb left in the nave and many in the transepts and choir.
- AD 1752 Henry Hindley's clock was installed in the south-west tower.
- AD 1815–37 Dilapidated houses in the vicinity cleared along with Ingram Mansion, High Minster Gates and Peter Prison. Dean Park created.
- AD 1824 Gas lighting installed.
- The Jonathan Martin fire, 1829.
- The William Groves fire, 1840.
- AD 1914 Windows removed for safety.
- AD 1940 Windows removed for safety, again.
- AD 1955 Astronomical Clock installed in memory of aircrew from northern airbases who lost their lives in the Second World War.
- AD 1966–73 Extensive work undertaken to underpin the foundations during which the Roman *principia* were revealed.

Hawkwind

On 18 July 1971, Hawkwind was the headline band in a free concert held in Museum Gardens.

4

York in 1972

The first known Royal Maundy took place in Knaresborough in 1210, during a visit by King John. Records, including *Rotulus Misae*, reveal that on 5 April 1210, *Die Jovis Cene* (the Day of the Lord's Supper), King John was staying at Knaresborough Castle and gave Maundy gifts of 13 pennies each to thirteen poor men of Knaresborough. The gifts were a robe, breeches, a girdle, a knife and shoes. The figure of thirteen is a reference to the number of diners at the Last Supper, not to the monarch's reign or age, as suggested by later tradition, although a red purse of money is still given 'in lieu of clothing'. On Good Friday, King John provided a meal for 100 Knaresborough paupers (costing 9s 4½d) and 1,000 more across Yorkshire (£4 13s 9d), both meals including bread and fish. *Rotulus Misae* is King John's account of his expenses (one of the oldest documents of its kind in existence), which proved beyond all doubt that he distributed Maundy gifts in Knaresborough in 1210. The extensive research leading to this conclusion was carried out by Arnold Kellett and is accepted by the Royal Almonry.

Henry IV began relating the number of recipients of gifts to the sovereign's age, and as it became the custom of the sovereign to perform the ceremony, the event became known as the Royal Maundy. For example, when the Queen was forty-six years old in 1972, forty-six women and forty-six men received 46-pence-worth of Maundy coins. In the eighteenth century, washing the feet of the poor was discontinued, and in the next century money allowances were substituted for gifts of food and clothing.

Maundy money started during the reign of Charles II with an undated issue of hammered coins in 1662. The coins were a four penny, three penny, two penny and one penny piece, but it was not until 1670 that a dated set of all four coins first appeared. Before this, everyday coinage was used for Maundy gifts, silver pennies alone being used by the Tudors and Stuarts for the ceremony. In 1971, decimalisation made it necessary to increase the face value of the coins from old to new pence.

Maundy Thursday commemorates the Last Supper of Jesus Christ with the Apostles after Jesus had washed their feet. The word 'Maundy' derives from the command or 'mandatum' by Christ at the Last Supper, 'that ye love one another' (John XIII 34).

Every year at Easter, the queen presents special 'Maundy Money' to local pensioners in a UK cathedral or abbey in recognition of the service of elderly people to their community and to their church. During the ceremony, the sovereign hands to each recipient two small leather string purses. One, a red purse, contains – in ordinary coinage – money in lieu of food and clothing; the other, a white purse, contains silver

Maundy coins consisting of the same number of pence as the years of the sovereign's age.

On 30 March 1972, the queen distributed the Maundy Money in York. Many of the women in the congregation wore Easter straw hats sporting scarlet roses. The scarlet was repeated in the medieval uniforms of the Yeoman of the Guard, the choir surplices, and the robes of the Aldermen and the Archbishop of York, Dr Donald Coggan. The path next to the Minster from Minster Yard to College Street was named The Queen's Path to commemorate her visit.

This is how the Court Circular described the day:

> The Queen, attended by the Hon Mary Morrison, Mr William Heseltine and Squadron Leader Peter Beer, arrived at York Central Railway Station this morning and was received by Her Majesty's Lieutenant for the West Riding of the County and for the City of York (Brigadier Kenneth Hargreaves) and the Lord Mayor (Alderman Richard Scruton). The Queen then drove to York Minster, was received by the Archbishop of York, and attended the Maundy Service at which Her Majesty distributed the Royal Maundy. The Queen subsequently honoured the Dean and Chapter with Her presence at luncheon in the Treasurer's House, Minster Court. This afternoon, Her Majesty inspected the work of restoration at York Minster, left Royal Air Force Rufforth in an aircraft of The Queen's Flight for Heathrow Airport, London, and drove to Windsor Castle.

In 2012, the ceremony was once again held in York Minster.

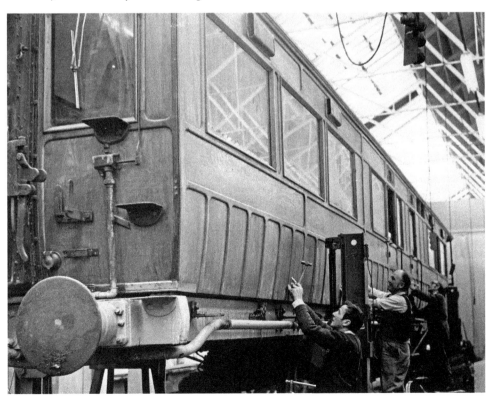

Restoration work at York carriage works, 27 January 1972.

The York Archaeological Trust

The Council for British Archaeology and the Yorkshire Philosophical Society sponsored the formation of the York Archaeological Trust (YAT) in April 1972 with funds from the Department of the Environment, and premises from York University. Its aim was to 'respond to the widespread threats to York's buried past posed by accelerated development. The Trust has been busy ever since, building upon a long tradition of exploration and preservation in the city'.

Its invaluable work involves excavation in advance of new building, and while trenches for gas, sewage and other services are dug. Significant contributions have, as a result, been made to our knowledge of the defences near the east corner in the Aldwark and Bedern area ahead of the urban regeneration proposed by Esher; work in Church Street in 1972 uncovered the great Roman sewer, which served the bathhouse; an excavation at No. 9 Blake Street in 1975 produced a row of Roman buildings and a street.

Across the Ouse, 1973 saw the excavation of a large town house on an artificial terrace in the south-eastern part of the settlement at No. 37 Bishophill Senior. Next door on the

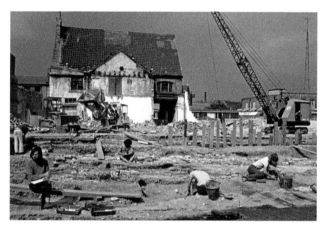

Archaeologists from YAT digging at Bedern Hall in the early 1970s.

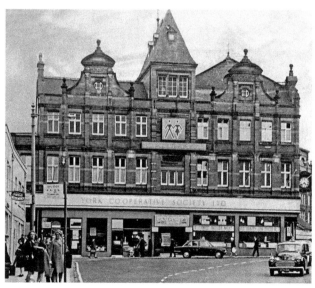

The Co-op in Rougier Street, 14 June 1972.

Nos 58–9 Skeldergate site a well-preserved timber-lined well was discovered, leading to the groundbreaking development of techniques for the treatment of waterlogged wood from archaeological sites; the Trust's conservation laboratory is now an internationally recognised centre of excellence for this work. The contents of the well were highly organic and included plant remains, animal bones and micro-organisms from the human gut, thus advancing our understanding of the ecology of the Roman settlement.

The York Archive Gazeteer is a record of nearly 1,000 excavations and watching briefs undertaken by the Trust since 1972. The gazeteer gives 'a brief description of the archaeology found at the sites and the type and period of the major archaeological features encountered'.

York Theatre Royal in 1972 – a Selection:

Mrs. Warren's Profession	George Bernard Shaw
The Glass Menagerie	Tennessee Williams
The Importance of Being Earnest	Oscar Wilde
The Tempest	William Shakespeare
It's Called the Sugar Plum	Israel Horowitz
Sootytime	
Sadler's Wells Opera	
Ghosts	Henrik Ibsen
Billy Liar	Keith Waterhouse & Willis Hall
The Birdwatcher	Georges Feydeau
Creditors	August Strindberg
Scottish Theatre Ballet	
Twelfth Night	William Shakespeare
The Circle	Somerset Maugham
Murder in the Cathedral	T. S. Eliot
Tiny Alice	Edward Albee
The Beggar's Opera (Phoenix Opera)	
The Cherry Orchard	Anton Chekhov
Welsh National Opera Company	
Christy in Love	Howard Brenton

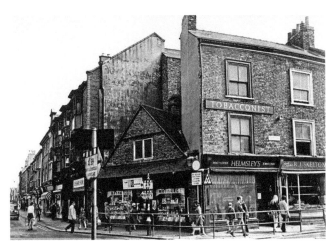

The corner of Gillygate and Bootham in 1972.

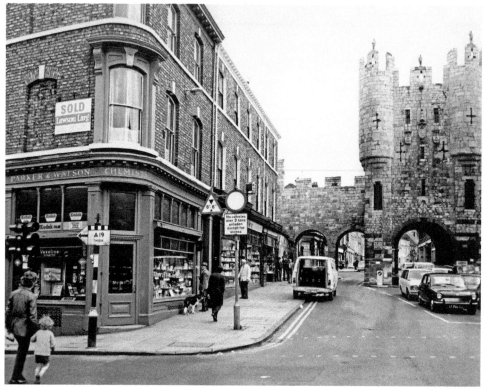

Micklegate in July 1972. Where's a traffic warden when you need one?

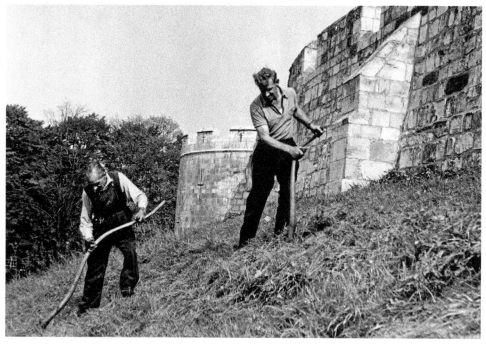

Les Nicolson and Bill Acomb scything the grass on the city walls on 8 September 1972.

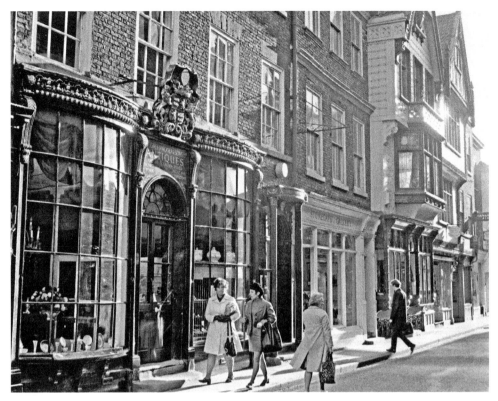

Stonegate in 1972; not that much has changed.

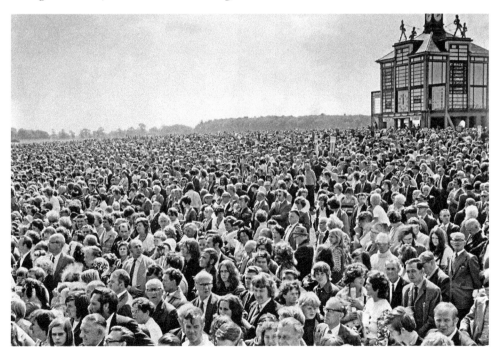

A day at the races for many in 1972.

5

YORK IN 1973

The Mystery Plays

The Mystery Plays were revived during the 1951 York Festival of the Arts; they were performed on a fixed stage in the Museum Gardens – it was not until 1954 that a wagon play, *The Flood,* toured the streets. The 1951 production was the most popular Festival of Britain event in the country, with over 26,000 people seeing the plays. The word 'mystery' in this context means a 'trade' or 'craft' in medieval English. It is also, of course, a religious truth or rite. The medieval plays were traditionally sponsored by the city's craft guilds – ninety-two separate trade associations – with an inclusive cast of 600 performers and 120 torchbearers, including the Lord Mayor, members of the council and ordinary folk; songs were in Latin. Richard II was in the audience in 1397; the last performance was in 1569. Nowadays, since 1994, the medieval *Corpus Christi* plays are produced every four years, with the latest in May 2016, for only the second time in their history performed in York Minster. *The Creation* to the *Last Judgement* is paraded through

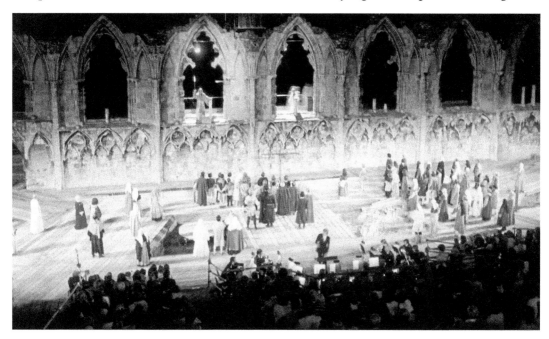

A floodlit performance of the Mystery Plays in the Museum Gardens.

the streets on pageant wagons as actors perform selections from the forty-eight high points of Christian history at twelve playing stations designated by the city banners, with one guild taking responsibility for one episode. The sole surviving manuscript of the York plays, from around 1465, is in the British Library.

The play was traditionally staged at two 'stations': the west front of York Minster and King's Square, one of the original medieval stations generally referred to as 'Girdlergate end' (Girdlergate is now Church Street). Between the two stations it processes along part of the old 'pageant route', which began on Pageant Green (Toft Green) and finished at Pavement. The wagon (or 'pageant') is drawn, as in the Middle Ages, by the gild presenting the play.

The wagon play for 1973 was *Herod and the Three Kings*, originally staged by the Masons and the Goldsmiths. The plot is that three kings come from the east, and Herod questions them about the child Jesus. The cast includes Herod's son and two counsellors and a messenger; Mary with the child, and the star above, and three kings offering gifts.

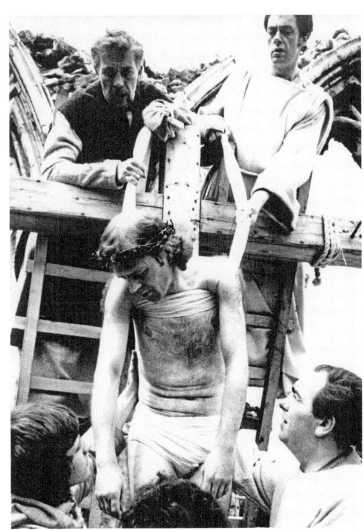

Jesus (John-Stuart Anderson) is lowered from the cross: 'The agony over, Christ's body is taken down from the cross by his faithful disciples'. (Courtesy of the Mystery Play archive at the National College of Early Music)

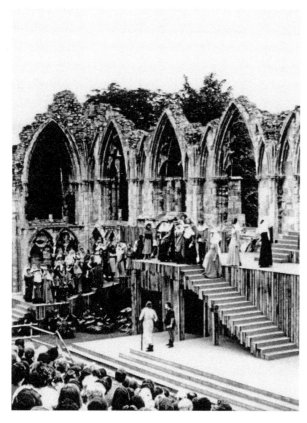

St Mary's Abbey makes a majestic backcloth for the Mystery Plays in the Museum Gardens. The plays are the centrepiece of the city's three-week festival. (Courtesy of the Mystery Play archive at the National College of Early Music)

York Celebrations Choir at the Festival

17 June, York Festival Concert, York Minster: *Psalm 103,* with Black Dyke Mills Band; *God Liveth Still,* Bach; *I will lay me down in peace,* Noble; *Down by the riverside,* Spiritual.

30 June, York Festival Concert, York Minster: *The Bells*, with New Philharmonia Orchestra, Rachmaninov. Concert also included Tchaikovsky's *Sixth Symphony.*

Eno Leaves Roxy in York

On 2 July 1973, Brian Eno left Roxy Music at the end of the New York Festival.

Over-enthusiastic Eno fans shouted over Ferry's vocals, which prompted Eno to leave the stage in an attempt to diffuse the situation. Ferry refused to confront Eno about the incident so Eno left the group. 'I was pissed off at the subterfuge and wanted Bryan to actually say it to my face,' said Eno, 'But he didn't. So eventually I just said, "OK f– it, I'm leaving."' The band officially announced his departure in *Melody Maker* on 21 July 1973.

Festival set list:
The Pride and the Pain
Do the Strand
Grey Lagoons

Beauty Queen
The Bogus Man
Ladytron
In Every Dreamhome a Heartache
If There Is Something
Editions of You
Pyjamarama
Virginia Plain

York Trade in 1973

Trade directories give us a reasonably accurate snapshot of the commercial climate in a town or city at any one time. *Kelly's Directory* for 1973 reveals the following more interesting businesses in the city:

2 blacksmiths: E. J. Dalby in Compton Street, J. Wedgwood in Holgate Road
1 bone setter: R. H. Stanley in Fulford Road
7 independent booksellers: Barbican Bookshop, Fossgate; Thomas Godfrey, Stonegate; R. Ogle, Colliergate; Pickering & Co, Shambles; Scrivener, Gillygate; Ken Spelman (second hand), Micklegate
2 brewers: Bass Charrington, Piccadilly; Yorkshire Club's Brewery, Huntington
1 brush manufacturer: Betterwear Products, Bridge Street
16 building societies
70 butchers
1 button manufacturer: Gansolite Ltd, Haxby Road
1 cattle dealer: Wm Abercrombie, Bleak House, Heslington Lane
20 coal merchants
3 convents: Bar Convent; St Wilfrid's, Heworth Green; Sisters of Charity of St Vincent de Paul, Fishergate
4 corsetieres: Mrs Edith Arey SRN, Cann Fit, Mrs Annie Martin, Mrs D. White
15 dairies
1 electrolysis operator
2 elocution teachers
2 French polishers
1 furrier
1 grinder and sharpener
1 gunsmith: Bulmer's, Lord Mayor's Walk
1 hide and skin merchant
1 horse slaughterer
16 hospitals
85 ladies' hairdressers
1 lemon curd manufacturer: Homemade Preserves, Barbican Road
5 midwives
2 potato merchants
1 trichologist
1 umbrella manufacturer
1 weaver
12 woolshops

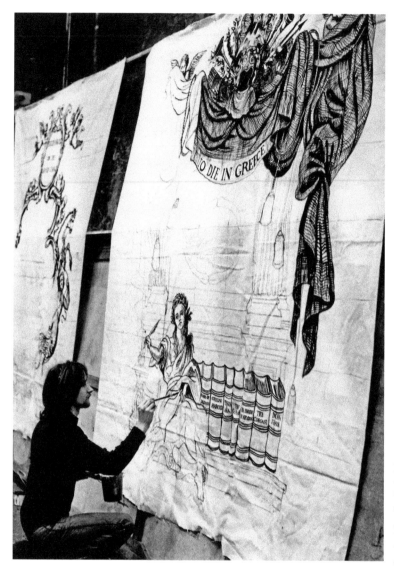

Kit Surrey
working on the
backcloths for the
Theatre Royal
production of
Lord Byron Lives,
January 1971.

York Theatre Royal in 1973 – a Selection:

Lord Byron Lives	Richard Digby Day
Servant of Two Masters	Carlo Goldoni
Hello Dolly (YLOS)	
The Corries in Concert	
The Secretary Bird	William Douglas Home
Gilbert & Sullivan for All	
Brief Lives	John Aubrey
The Royal Ballet	
Jake Thackray	
Janet Baker Recital	

The Settlers in Concert
The Happiest Days of Your Life John Dighton
Hay Fever Noel Coward
Fiddler on the Roof (YAODS)
The Trial of Joan of Arc Gerald McLarnon
Sadler's Wells Opera
Love on the Dole Ronald Gow & Walter Greenwood
Arms and the Man George Bernard Shaw
Two Noble Kinsmen
There's a Girl in My Soup Terence Frisby
All Over Edward Albee
The Rivals By (Harrogate Co.) Richard Brinsley Sheridan
Richard III William Shakespeare
Max Jaffa
Home David Storey
Labi Siffre
Le Misanthrope Moliere
How the Other Half Loves Alan Ayckbourn
Johnny Dankworth

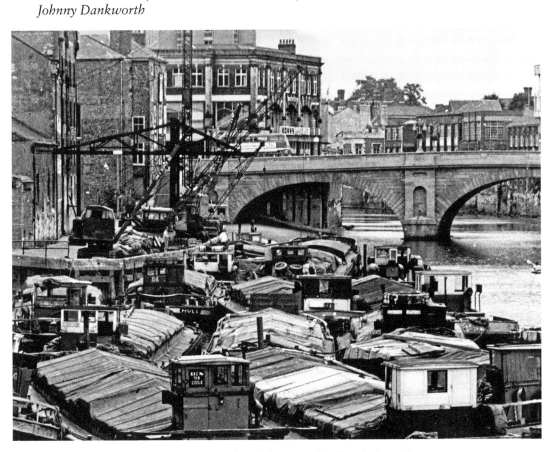

A busy September day on Queen's Staith with barges unloading their goods.

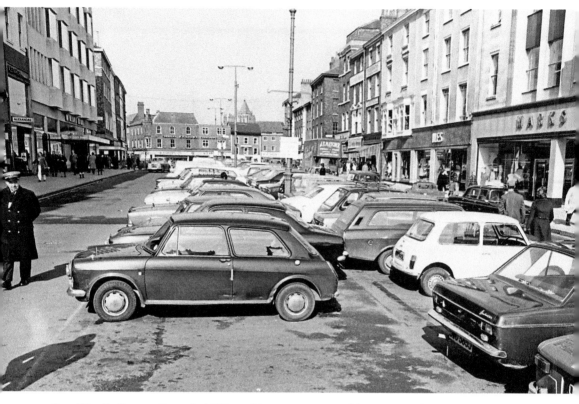

Patrolling Parliament Street in 1973; parking came to an end here in March 1974.

6

YORK IN 1974

York, like everywhere else in Yorkshire, was affected by local government reforms in 1974. Under the Local Government Act 1972, the ridings lost their historic lieutenancies and shrievalties and the former administrative counties, county boroughs and their councils were abolished. Yorkshire was carved up between a number of metropolitan and non-metropolitan counties.

York was to become part of North Yorkshire, which, from 1974, comprised the city of York, most of the North Riding, Harrogate, Knaresborough and Selby imported from the West Riding, and part of the East Riding around Filey. On Teesside, Yorkshire's Middlesbrough, Stockton and Redcar were moved into the new county of Cleveland along with Hartlepool from County Durham.

The map had been well and truly redrawn, and some York councillors resigned rather than sit on what they saw as an emasculated body, stripped of its power, dignity and rights.

York had had its own charter since in 1212, when King John allowed York's citizens, rather than the sheriff, to collect and pay the annual tax to the Crown, to hold their own courts and to appoint a mayor. From then on, until local government reorganisation in 1974, York was a self-governing city and a county borough under its own mayors. In 1835, York was reformed by the Municipal Corporations Act to form a municipal borough. It gained the status of a county borough in 1889, under the Local Government Act 1888, and existed so until 1974, when, under the Local Government Act 1972, it became a non-metropolitan district in the county of North Yorkshire with powers relating to social services, education, planning and so on, ceded to North Yorkshire County Council in Northallerton.

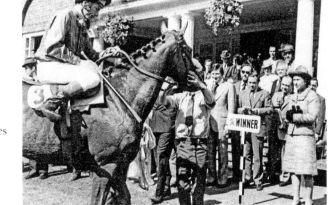

May 1974: a day at the races. The queen attended York Races several times in the 1970s. Here she is in 1974 watching Lester Piggott dismount from Escorial after winning the Musidora Stakes.

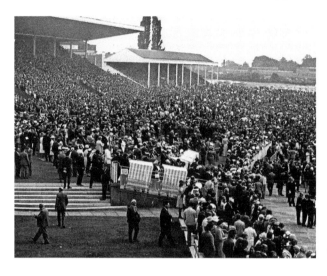

The Ebor Meeting in 1974.

York, though, was a special case: in recognition of its special historic status, the queen by charter allowed it to retain its city status, and keep the office of sheriff and the chairman of the council to be called the Right Honourable the Lord Mayor. Apart from the Lord Mayors of London, Belfast and Cardiff, all other Lord Mayors are addressed as the 'Worshipful'.

The office of Lord Mayor remains, of course, the highest accolade the city of York can bestow on one of its citizens. In 1978/79, Mayor Sam Brearley inaugurated a Tree Fund to restore York's green-ness and urged planners to build more car parks in the city centre, but in discrete locations. Seems like a couple of contradictions.

York Theatre Royal in 1974 – a Selection:

The Soldier's Tale	Igor Stravinsky
Gilbert and Sullivan for All	
1974 Rock and Roll Show	
Bell, Book & Candle	John Van Druden
David Kossoff	
The Philanthropist	Christopher Hampton
Ralph McTell	
Chris Barber's Jazz Band	
Scottish Opera	
New London Ballet	
Dangerous Corner	J. B. Priestley
Donald Swann	
Carousel (YAODS)	Rodgers & Hammerstein
Stephane Grappelli	
Dance of Death	Strindberg
Suddenly at Home	Francis Durbridge
Getting Married	George Bernard Shaw
Lloyd George Knew My Father	William Douglas Home
Arsenic and Old Lace	Joseph Kesselring
The Settlers	

Entertaining Mr. Sloane	Joe Orton
The Flamenco Playa Dance Company of Madrid	
Waiting for Godot	Samuel Beckett
A Man for All Seasons	Robert Bolt
Los Paraguayos	
King's Singers	
La Vie Parisienne (Phoenix Opera)	
Equus	Peter Shaffer
Hassan performed by National Theatre for the Deaf	
Hamlet	William Shakespeare
Paradise Lost (York Archaeological Trust)	
Sense of Detachment	John Osborne

St Sampson's Church Converted

Now 'St Sampson's Centre for the Over 1960s' – a bustling day centre for senior citizens since 1974 with tea dances held every other month. The *Yorkshire Evening Press*, in a leader on 16 November 1974, described the centre as 'one of the happiest and most imaginative of schemes York has seen for many a day ... Here is a place where the elderly can meet socially in comfort and above all find friendship and relief from the loneliness which can be the worst affliction of their age group.' It owes its origins to the then Archbishop of York, Dr Donald Coggan, who was appalled by the sight of so many elderly, retired men sitting on benches in the centre of York; he felt it was disgraceful that all these men were sitting outside with nowhere to go. The Civic Trust rose to the challenge and took the building over (it had been redundant since 1968); the centre was opened by Queen Elizabeth the Queen Mother in November 1974. The building was sensitively restored in such a way that the original historic fabric remained unaltered. While having tea at the opening ceremony, the Queen Mother sat down with the archbishop and was approached by an elderly lady. 'Ma'am you should put some rum in it,' she said while stroking her expansive bosom, 'it will make you feel warm all over.'

St Sampson's Church is the only church in the country dedicated to St Sampson. According to Geoffrey of Monmouth's *History of the Kings of Britain*, he was installed by King Arthur's uncle, Ambrosius Aurelianus, as Archbishop of York after repelling a force of Saxon invaders in AD 466. This Sampson, of course, has nothing to do with the famous Samson in the Bible – he of the long hair and Delilah.

The church was built into the wall of the old Roman fortress. A fragment of a cross-shaft from the first half of the eleventh century, found built into a house in Newgate on the corner of Patrick Pool within the former churchyard, suggests a pre-Conquest date for the earliest church, but in 1974, the York Archaeological Trust uncovered a stone wall that appeared to be Norman. St Sampson's was extensively rebuilt in the 1400s. In 1336, licence was granted for a chantry row of 'rental houses' to finance the chantry of the Virgin Mary. Between seven and ten two-storey, one room per floor jettied and timber-framed buildings were erected; five survive at Nos 12–15 Newgate.

St Sampson Girdlegate (to give its full name) is first mentioned in 1154 when it was granted to Pontefract Priory. By 1226, it was in the hands of the Archdeacon of Richmond; in 1394, Richard II gave the church to the Vicars Choral of York

Minster, where it remained until 1936. The tower was badly damaged, 'shot through and through', by cannon fire during the Civil War Siege of York in 1644. The parliamentarians followed this by iconclasm, which 'left us not so much as a tomb, monument or gravestone'. By 1844, it was damaged by fire and had become so dilapidated that it closed and, in 1848, was pulled down allowing a new church to be built. This closed in 1969 when furnishings were removed to All Saints Pavement and James the Deacon in Acomb.

In 1847, Alfred Hargrove gloomily described the churchyard as follows in his *The Baneful Custom of Interment in Towns*: 'as is well known [it] adjoins the fish market. It contains about 30 perches and is in such a disgusting state, that no interments can take place without interfering with human remains ... it is so wet and swampy that graves have been known to be partly filled with water ... and when the coffin has been lowered, it has plunged out of sight into a mass of loathsome mire whilst the mourners have shuddered around'.

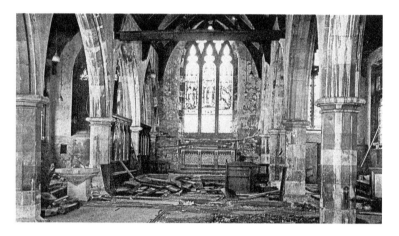

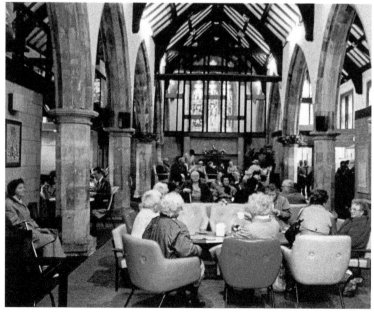

St Sampson's before and after restoration.

7

YORK IN 1975

The National Railway

The history and origins of the National Railway Museum at York go back to the Railway Centenary Exhibition that was held in York in 1925, the success of which led to the opening of the first Railway Museum in 1927, in Queen Street.

The Science Museum in London – known then as the Patent Office Museum – tentatively started the country's collection of railway locomotives by buying *Rocket* (in 1866), *Puffing Billy*, and *Agenoria*, the oldest locomotive in the world, in such pristine condition, and sister locomotive to *Stourbridge Lion*, exported to the USA in 1829 and the first locomotive to run on rails there.

The North Eastern Railway then opened the public Railway Museum in Queen Street, once a repair shop attached to the original Motive Power Department. It was chosen in preference to the old plumber's shop behind the passenger station. Initially, the museum was somewhat exclusive – open only to invited guests and VIPs in the industry; January 1928 saw the doors open to the public. The first exhibit was a wooden ticket dating press. Around the same time, a multitude of small exhibits was removed from the Headquarters of the London & North Eastern Railway and displayed in the first-class refreshment room in the old station. They remained there until 1966 when they were finally moved to Queen Street. During the Second World War, many of the large exhibits were dispersed to less vulnerable locations. A branch of British Transport Historical Records was set up at York in 1955 to facilitate railway related research. In 1958, an exhibition of royal coaches opened.

By the 1930s, all the railway companies had ad hoc railway-related collections of relics with little effort going in to centralisation; these collections were only combined in 1948 after Nationalisation. Things, however, from 1961, were gravitating away from York towards the Transport Commission's Museum of British Transport in a converted bus garage in Clapham. Their collection included the restored *Mallard*; 200,000 people per year visited the museum. Other railway museums existed at Swindon GWR Museum and at Glasgow Transport Museum.

The Beeching Report recommended that British Rail should wash its hands of museums, resulting in a campaign to create a new national museum. Under the terms of the 1968 Transport Act, a National Railway Museum was to be set up at York as a branch of the National Museum of Science and Industry, there being no room at South Kensington. It was to be the first English national museum outside London, established to house the expanding collection, then located in Clapham, and in the existing York Railway Museum at Queen Street. The Transport Act also usefully ordained that the museum had first claim on redundant items from British Rail without cost.

York's National Railway Museum gives us another salvo in the ongoing battle of the north–south divide. Xenophobic southerners were incredulous that a national museum

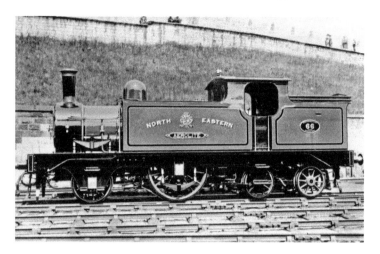

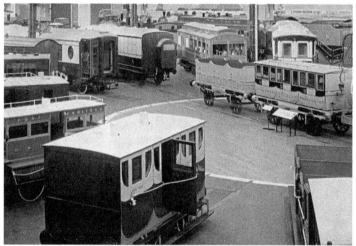

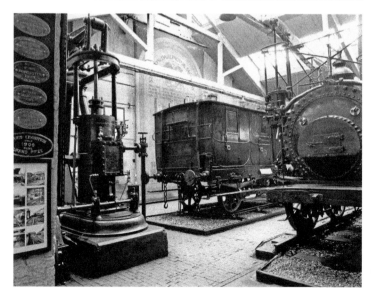

A selection of Queen Street exhibits.

could be located outside London. They were led by Lord Montague of Beaulieu, who tabled a special debate in the House of Lords arguing that it was inconceivable that any visitor to the UK would want to go all that way to the provinces to visit a museum, not least one in York. *The Times* and, ironically, the Duke of Edinburgh, were on the side of Lord Montague. A petition was signed by 122 MPs desperate to keep the museum in London. Peterborough, Harrow and Crystal Palace were all in the race as possible venues. The flat-earth MPs, though, were outgunned by people power: a 90,000 petition in favour of York was influential, as was a visionary Jenny Lee, Labour MP.

York, of course, won the day. Conversion work started: Queen Street closed on New Year's Eve, 1973; Clapham had closed in April that year. On 27 September 1975, the celebrated National Railway Museum was opened at Leeman Road in York by the once anti-Duke of Edinburgh himself. But not before divine retribution played a hand: British Rail laid on a High Speed Diesel Train (HSDT) – the prototype of the Intercity 125 – to get the duke to York. However, one of the power units caught fire at Welwyn Garden City, and, unbeknown to a sleeping national press, proceeded at a leisurely 105 mph, making him late for the ceremony.

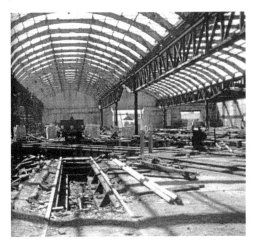

The engine shed being converted into what became the Great Hall in 1974.

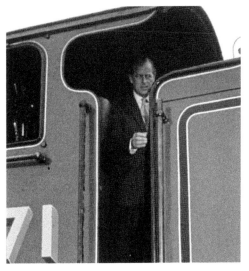

The Duke of Edinburgh during the opening ceremony on the footplate of LNER V2 locomotive No. 4771 named *Green Arrow*.

Some of the main locomotive exhibits in 1975:

1829 Shutt End Railway 0-4-0 *Agenoria*
1845 GJR 2-2-2 No. 49 *Columbine*
1846 Furness Railway 0-4-0 *Old Coppernob*
1869 NER 2-2-4 tank No. 66 *Aerolite*
1882 LBSCR 0-4-2 No. 214 *Gladstone*
1938 LNER 4-6-2 No. 4468 *Mallard*
1941 SR 4-6-2 No. 35029 *Ellerman Lines* (sectioned)
1960 BR 2-10-0 No. 92220 *Evening Star*

Some of the main rolling stock exhibits in 1975:

1797 Peak Forest Canal quarry truck
1816 Grantham Canal Wharf tramway truck
1842 LABR Queen Adelaide's coach
1869 LNWR royal saloon for Queen Victoria
1885 WCJS travelling post office
1903 royal saloon for King Edward VII
1906 NER dynamometer car

The building from which it rose was the converted old York North engine shed, originally opened by the North Eastern Railway in 1878 and rebuilt in 1958, alongside the East Coast Main Line. It was known as the North Motive Power Depot and housed four locomotive turntables, the largest of which measures 21.5 m and is still delighting visitors when in action in the Great Hall. The date coincided with the 150th anniversary of the opening of the Stockton & Darlington Railway. Around 500,000 people passed through the doors in the first two months of its opening with over 2 million in the first

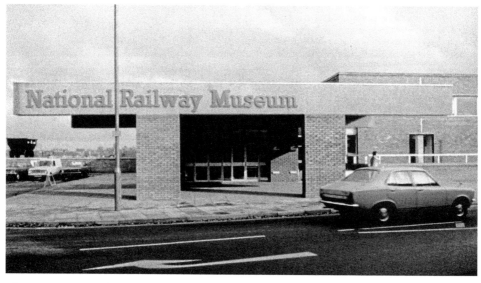

The museum soon after its opening in 1975. A chaldron wagon can be seen on the left, on top of the Gaunless Bridge, the first iron railway bridge in the world.

twelve months. Admission was free. The continuing scepticism of southern-based civil servants who spectacularly underestimated the appeal of a northern-based national museum resulted in a woefully inadequate cafeteria, but apart from that everything went extremely well.

The year 1979 saw the restoration of a train of vehicles to mark the centenary of on-train catering and an exhibition to mark the centenary of railway electric traction. Also in 1979, the museum commissioned a working replica of Stephenson's *Rocket* for the Liverpool & Manchester Railway's 150th anniversary in 1980.

The museum displays over 100 locomotives and 300 other items of rolling stock, most of which either ran on the railways of Great Britain or were built there. Also on the 20-acre site are many hundreds of thousands of other railway-related items of social, technical, artistic and historical interest. The museum had 727,000 visitors in the 2014/15 financial year. The largest railway museum in the world in terms of floor area is La Cité du Train in Mulhouse, France, although this attracts significantly fewer visitors than the National Railway Museum.

The York museum boasts a unique display of royal railway vehicles, or 'palaces on wheels', indeed the best of its kind in the world. This started when a member of staff at the London & North Western Railway works at Wolverton fortuitously salvaged the royal saloon there from destruction. It had been used by Queen Adelaide Amelia Louisa Theresa Caroline, sister of the Duke of Saxe-Meiningen and widow of King William IV before her death in 1849. From then on many of the royal saloons of subsequent monarchs and their families have been preserved and are now in York, in all their splendour.

The 8-foot-10-inch-diameter railway wheels at the entrance to the museum are probably the largest locomotive wheels in existence; they were cast at Bristol in 1873 to drive 4-2-4 Tender Loco No. 40, an express passenger train of the Bristol & Exeter

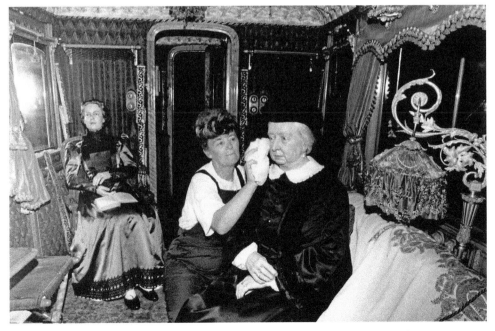

How would Victoria have taken to being an 'object'? She certainly was not a 'subject'.

Railway. The wheels have been part of the National Railway Collection since 1964 and have been in their present location since 1975.

In 1994, the Institute of Railway Studies was launched as a joint venture between the National Railway Museum and York University. In 1999, *The Works* was opened, effectively expanding the museum to three times its original size. The museum won the European Museum of the Year award in 2001. In 2004, the Yorkshire Rail Academy, a purpose-built rail training centre and the base for the museum's education team, was opened. It was a joint development between York College and the museum. The latest development is Search Engine, the £4 million archive and research centre that gives public access to previously unseen artwork, papers, reports, photographs and artefacts. Search Engine is one of the largest and richest collections of railway-related material in the world. It holds 1.75 or so million photographs covering the earliest days of photography to the present day. These include official

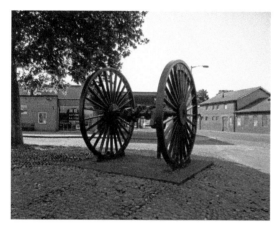

The Museum's big wheels.

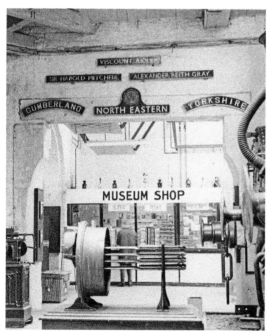

The museum shop at Queen Street.

collections from railway companies and collections from aficionados like Eric Treacy and H. Gordon Tidey.

On 23 September 2015, Virgin Trains East Coast and the National Railway Museum joined forces to celebrate four decades of the museum's life. Locomotive No. 43238 was renamed *National Railway Museum 40 Years 1975–2015* on the platform at York station.

The same locomotive was previously called *National Railway Museum – The First Ten Years 1975–1985* for twelve years from 1985. It now bears a distinctive and specially designed livery, showing major exhibits from the museum's collection, including the working replica of Stephenson's *Rocket* and *Locomotion No. 1* currently on loan to Darlington's Head of Steam Railway Museum.

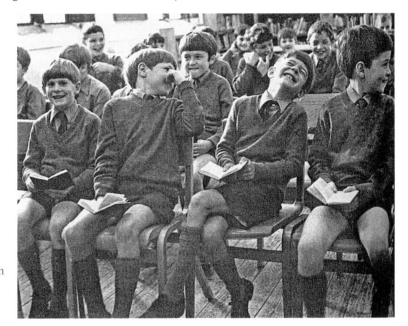

Non-choristers in a singing lesson at the Minster School in 1975.

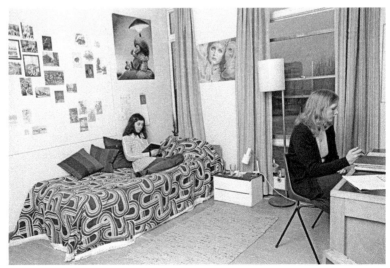

Student bedroom at Langwith College at the University of York in 1975. Note the BIBA poster.

Joseph Rowntree (24 May 1836 – 24 February 1925)

24 February 1975 saw the 50th anniversary of the death of Joseph Rowntree, one of, if not the, greatest of York's sons.

Joseph, when he left school in 1852, aged sixteen, began an apprenticeship at the Pavement shop where, it seems, he was treated just like any other apprentice, along with George Cadbury and one of the Fry boys. The rules of the Pavement shop were uncompromising, as set out in his father's, also Joseph, 1852 *Memoranda of Business and Household Arrangements*:

> The object of the Pavement establishment is business. The young men who enter it ... are expected to contribute ... in making it successful ... it affords a full opportunity for any painstaking, intelligent young man to obtain a good practical acquaintance with the tea and grocery trades ... the place is not suitable for the indolent and wayward.

Pavement was to furnish Joseph Rowntree with a sound and invaluable seventeen-year apprenticeship in retail and business management, with special relevance to the grocery business. This, and an earlier period of work as a wholesale grocer's near Fenchurch Street in London from 1857, provided a priceless foundation for the next stage of his career when he joined his brother Henry Isaac at the cocoa works in Tanner's Moat.

Joseph, when he made the move from Pavement to Tanner's Moat, probably realised that he was at the point of no return with his career: he described himself on his third child's birth certificate in 1875 no longer as a 'master grocer', which was his wont until now, but as a 'cocoa manufacturer'. Grocery was the trade in which he had spent all of his working life so far; cocoa and chocolate were to be his life from now on.

A felicitous combination of Joseph's meticulousness, increased product lines and a rise in demand raised the company's fortunes. Rowntrees were, of course, at the mercy of market trends: cocoa prices fell from 1873 to 1879, signifying something of a depression, and foreign competition was increasing from the French, Dutch and Swiss. But, on the other hand, between 1870 and 1890 cocoa consumption in the UK increased from nearly 7 million pounds weight to over 20 million pounds with a rise in consumption per capita from 0.22 pounds weight to 0.53.

Homoeopathic Cocoa was launched in 1876, riding on the medicinal properties ascribed to arrowroot. More diverse lines included a granular effervescent citrate of magnesia fruit sauce; Rowntree also secured the agency for Neaves' Farinaceous Infant Food – competition for Nestlé, the current market leader in this field.

A man called Hanks ran the chocolate cream department assisted by one girl; Hanks was also nightwatchman (he lived next door to the factory) and was wages clerk. His own wages would have been around 16s per week. 'No man then had any specific job – even the few clerks had at times to take off their coats for labouring work.' This musical-chairs staffing model persisted into the 1880s and 1890s, yet it did give opportunities for promotion: an employee originally hired as a timekeeper moved on to general manager and then took charge of the mélangeur and cake room departments. Another man, hired as a junior clerk, transferred to the cream rooms as manager to twenty staff; on retirement, he was responsible for nearly 1,000 workers. Departmentalisation began in around 1896, driven by the special needs of pastille production. By the mid-1890s, there were managers for storerooms, packing, the railway, drawing office and engineering. In 1862, there had been twelve staff; over 100 in 1880; 900 in 1894; and 4,000 in 1910.

The prize acquisition, though, was undoubtedly the van Houten press; this enabled the production and launch in 1880 of cocoa essence – Rowntrees Elect, 'more than a drink, a food', made from top-quality cocoa. The name 'Elect' came from the apothecary trade where it was used to signify an especially efficacious drug. Elect was 'an extremely light powder, the essential product of the cocoa bean after it had been roasted and ground and the fat (cocoa butter) taken out by hydraulic pressure'. But, despite the new press and an increase in demand, output remained low: in 1893, Elect still only accounted for 6 per cent of sales and 2.5 per cent of output; profits remained unimpressive at 2.5 per cent of turnover in 1888.

A serendipitous sales call by Claude Gaget in 1879 had a significant and lasting impact on Rowntrees. Gaget at the time was working in the London office of Compagnie Française, Parisian confectioners specialising in gums and pastilles – sweets that, up until then, were the exclusive preserve of French manufacturers. The samples he presented to Henry and Joseph that day eventually led to the manufacture of their famous Crystallized Gum Pastilles in 1881. Gaget was soon on board, in charge of the newly created French Confectionery Department where he perfected Almond Paste, but it was only after two years of anxious and frustrating experimentation, during which Joseph Rowntree at one stage threatened to throw Gaget's work into the River Ouse, that production began of Crystallized Gum Pastilles that were of the highest quality but sellable at a realistic retail price.

However, the relative success of fruit pastilles enabled Joseph to buy more property and machinery in 1880: a refrigerator and much-needed, more efficient machines for cleaning the beans and turning out the nibs. Property was purchased in nearby Queen Street – and the North Street flour mill (Simpson's flour mill purchased in 1882) and the Tanner's Moat cottages were extended and refurbished. Things were still decidedly rudimentary though: there was one joiner working from what can only be described as a hutch measuring 8 feet by 6; in engineering, there was one man equipped with a hammer, chisel and files. North Street now had six storeys, but no lift.

The jumble of improvised buildings at Henry's Tanner's Moat, which would have greeted Joseph, was nothing if not full of character. Apart from the resident parrot, there was a somewhat temperamental donkey obedient to one man and one man only, and a serious danger to everyone else. On its dismissal, deliveries were relegated to a handcart. Night-shift workers were sustained by cocoa and pork pies on the firm, and most communications to and from Joseph Rowntree were through a trapdoor in the floor of his Lendal Bridge-facing office. Hanks, the foreman, paid the wages each Saturday from a hat full of silver and coppers (£60 a week usually covered it); each employee would be asked 'how much time has thee got?' and duly paid his or her going rate from the contents of the hat. Mistakes were inevitably made, which prompted 'What did I give thee?' Girls aged around fourteen would have earned around 3s per week, boys a shilling more; men earned 18s at most – fairly standard money for the times. The purchase of a horse and wagonette in 1874 proved injudicious – an overhead the company could ill afford: food, farriers' and veterinary bills, and tolls amounted to 12s and 7d three farthings per week. The horse was duly sold and the wagonette mothballed. Factory production was steam driven but hampered by the use of different machines for each of the processes involved (grinding, sifting, roasting etc.) with raw materials laboriously manhandled between machines. Hours were long: Monday to Saturday, 6 a.m. to 6 p.m. or 2 p.m. on Saturdays. Indeed, Tanner's Moat was inadequate. Seebohm Rowntree said of it: 'Tanner's Moat was Hell.' Coming from a man not usually given over to such language, these were strong words indeed.

In 1890, Joseph followed suite when he bought a 29-acre site to the north of York on Haxby Road. The objective: to build a highly efficient and ergonomic factory that would improve production techniques and transportation to meet the growing demand for their products in a pleasant working environment. In Joseph's own words, he desired a workplace where his workforce could 'develop all that is best and worthy in themselves'. Indeed 'healthful conditions of labour are not luxuries to be adopted or dispensed at will. They are conditions necessary for success'. Joseph was 'determined to spare neither pains nor money to incorporate the most complete and modern arrangements ... for manufacturing purposes'.

Tanner's Moat had been inadequate in every way. The new factory would be an efficient and convivial workplace with pleasant garden areas. And so it transpired: offices were lit by electricity powered by a generator; the factory benefitted from its own North Eastern Railway branch line from Foss Islands and a halt. There was a library and two savings bank were opened, one for men and one for women. All manner of clubs and societies were funded by the company. The Fruit Room and Gum Department were the first to move over in 1893, and by 1898, all production was on the new site.

So began the career of Joseph Rowntree – architect of one of the world's greatest companies, Quaker and benefactor extraordinaire.

York Theatre Royal in 1975 – a Selection:

Dracula	Bram Stoker
Verdict	Agatha Christie
Royal Ballet	
The Dancing Years	Ivor Novello
Syd Lawrence Orchestra	
Little Eyolf	Henrik Ibsen
Ralph McTell	
Scottish Opera	
The Threepenny Opera	Bertolt Brecht & Kurt Weill
Cleo Laine and Johnny Dankworth	
Labbi Siffre	
Time and Time Again	Alan Ayckbourn
Emlyn Williams as Charles Dickens	
The Two Gentlemen of Verona	William Shakespeare
Not I	Samuel Beckett
The Maids	Jean Genet
Pygmalion	George Bernard Shaw
Dear Octopus	Dodie Smith
Habeas Corpus	Alan Bennett
Raymond Villar Flamenco Dance Company	

The Dubliners
The Merchant of Venice   William Shakespeare
Stephane Grappelli & Diz Disley
The Lion in Winter   James Goldman
Tribute to Edith Piaf   Madlena Buznea
Under Milk Wood   Dylan Thomas
Shrivings   Peter Shaffer
Syd Lawrence Orchestra
Bournemouth Sinfonietta
Joseph and the Amazing Technicolor Dreamcoat

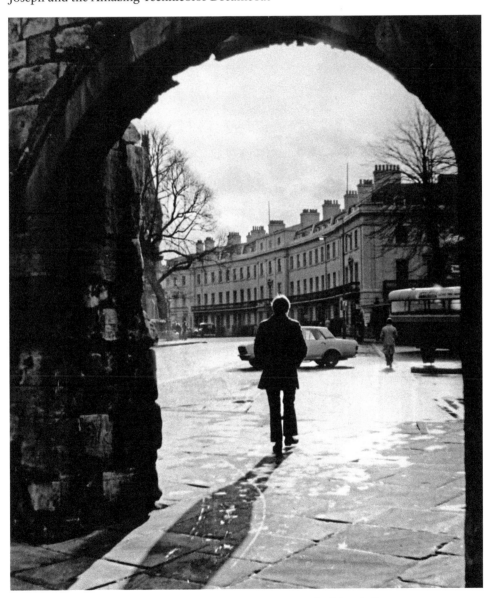

The curve of St Leonard's Place framed by Queen Margaret's Arch in 1975.

8

York in 1976

Digging up the Vikings

Astonishingly perhaps, the only significant archaeological finds in York before the 1970s were dug up by accident. But this started to change in 1972 when small exploratory trenches near Lloyds Bank in Pavement were excavated by York Archaeological Trust (YAT). These test digs revealed some truly exciting facts.

Unusually, there was up to 9 m of archaeological layers dating mostly to the Viking Age. These layers were both waterlogged and peaty – excellent preservatives for the organic remains of timber buildings, textiles from clothing and leather shoes, things that rot away and turn to dust on most archaeological sites. It was all buried under the accumulation of 2 cm per year of sludge and domestic trash. The moist peaty layers also preserved seeds, insect remains, plants, animal bones, human parasite eggs and pollen, providing unparalleled evidence about climate, diet, health, personal hygiene and other features of the excavated environment.

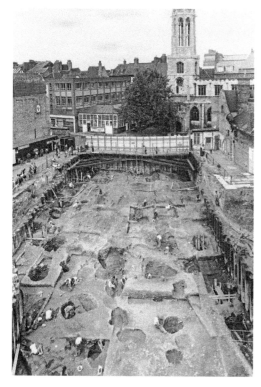

The Jorvik dig site with All Saints in the background and the old cornmarket.

With the announcement of the Coppergate development in 1976 on the site of Craven's sweet factory, YAT had an opportunity to dig deeper, as it were. In May of that year, a number of modern basements were excavated, and very soon rare traces of Viking-Age timber buildings, some up to 2 m high, were exposed. The area of excavation was over 1,000 square metres, giving unparalleled access to 2,000 years of York's history.

Between 1976 and 1981, YAT identified and recorded around 40,000 items. The excavation team comprised around twelve professional excavators, along with students from all over the world, local amateur archaeologists and inmates of HM Prisons on day release. According to the Jorvik Viking Centre website, the site revealed the following:

- 5 tons of animal bones – mostly the remains of food eaten here over the centuries
- vast quantities of oyster shells – until recently a cheap and common food
- Thousands of Roman and medieval roof tiles; the Roman tiles were sometimes reused for other purposes in the Viking Age
- woven wattles, used as building materials to make walls, pathways and screens
- timber used for building materials in both the Viking Age and medieval periods
- metalworking slag – vital evidence showing technology over the centuries
- a quarter of a million pieces of pottery; pieces that can be used for dating, showing where the pots were made and what they were used for
- several tons of soil were sieved through to recover tiny objects and microscopic environmental evidence, 2,500 soil samples were recorded for further analysis, and thousands of timbers were conserved for long-term preservation
- 20,000 individually interesting objects were also unearthed (http://jorvik-viking-centre.co.uk/about-jorvik/the-coppergate-dig/ accessed 12 December 2015)

Fascinating revelations included groundbreaking information that has added immeasurably to our knowledge of Roman and Saxon York, but particularly to our understanding of the Viking era. The dig yielded up priceless details regarding

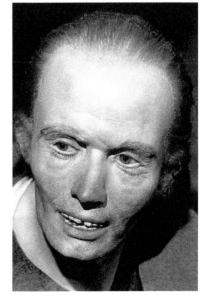

One of the vivid reconstructions that has come out of the excavations. Meet Eymund in the Jorvik Viking exhibit. He was born around AD 948 and is reconstructed from a male skeleton unearthed in a Viking cemetery in Fishergate.

the construction and layout of the buildings in which the Vikings lived and worked, commercial activities and the manufacture of goods, the diet of the Vikings, and how they spent their time at work and in leisure.

The houses had a central fire making them warm and very smoky. Two layers of timber planks formed the wall insulated with twigs. Wooden planks outside made paths, and there were twig fences between the houses. Toilets, or cesspits, were holes in the ground.

The four wattle tenements from the tenth century excavated at Coppergate saw little change over the next few years. Metalworkers lived in two of them, one of whom also minted coins – the first mint of this period ever found. Near the end of the century, all the houses were replaced with plank-built, partly sunken buildings within the same property boundaries. The metalworkers had left to be replaced with a jeweller and a wood-turner. As before, the backyards were used for craft activities, storage, privies and waste disposal, all of which left tantalising and fascinating finds for the archaeologists of the YAT.

Finds of coins and jewellery suggest a certain level of wealth and some commerce, with a silk hat from the Middle East and a decorative sea shell from the Red Sea.

Academic interest apart, it was vital that all this historical evidence be made accessible to the public at large. Its educational value was huge, and it represented a unique leap forward in our knowledge of Viking York and of the Vikings in Britain generally. Thus was born the seeds of the Jorvik Viking Centre that opened in 1984.

> Design and construction began in 1981, with the intention of creating a historic attraction that was more like the set of a film. Instead of walking around looking at exhibits, the visitor would sit in specially designed time-cars, and move around the 'set' of a Viking village, taking it in from all angles, and witnessing Viking life up-close.

Much of the attraction is set in the year AD 975, the 1,000th anniversary of which was in 1975.

Jorvik is the Viking name for York. It all started when the Viking army attacked the city on 1 November AD 866 under the command of Halfdan and Ivar the Boneless. The timing and date were no coincidence, it being All Saints Day when much of the population would have been preoccupied worshipping in the old cathedral. York soon became the capital of the Viking kingdom in the north. In AD 954, the last Viking king, Eric Bloodaxe, was expelled. Ivar was boneless on account of his chubby face – nothing to do with an absence of skeleton. He was the son of Ragnar Lothbrok. The Coppergate Dig and the resulting Jorvik Viking Centre opens a unique and fascinating window on the world of the Vikings during those years and changed the way we look at the Viking Age.

Some essential facts about the Vikings:

- Their conquests included modern-day western Turkey, Ireland, Normandy, Iceland, Greenland and Newfoundland.
- They boasted interesting nicknames like Harald Bluetooth and Sihtric the Squinty.
- They have the reputation for being inveterate rapists and pillagers. A bit of a stereotype; for example, in York they embraced Christianity and were great civilisers.
- Political links between Scandinavia and Britain only came to an end in 1469 when Orkney and Shetland were returned by the Norwegian king to the Scots.
- Vikings take their name from the area known as Viki in Oslo Fjord.

- By the year 1000, the Scandinavian kingdoms of Denmark, Norway and Sweden had been created as smaller chiefdoms were merged. Christianity had also become established, and soon after his death in 1030 King Olaf of Norway had become St Olaf, with churches dedicated to him in York, London, and elsewhere.
- The last Scandinavian king was Harald Hardrada of Norway, who had served in the bodyguard of Byzantium emperors, and was eventually killed at Stamford Bridge in 1066.

Public Inconvenience

Public conveniences have often been a source of controversy in York. On 12 April 1976, no fewer than seven public conveniences were unceremoniously flushed away due to cost, lack of usage (how was that observed without the observers being arrested?), maintenance and vandalism. The toilets in question were at Baile Hill, Blue Bridge Lane, Dennis Street, Fourth Avenue, Melrosegate, Micklegate Bar and Walmgate Bar. The council gave York residents three months in which to lodge complaints, but only eight people bothered.

The Mystery Plays

The second of two productions of the Mystery Plays was staged in the 1970s. York actor David Bradley played Jesus in 1976. Bradley went on to star as Argus Filch in the *Harry Potter* films, and Walder Frey in *Game of Thrones*, also starring in *Our Friends in the North*, and *Broadchurch*.

He was educated at the Catholic St George's Secondary Modern School where he was a member of the choir, first performing on stage with the Rowntree Youth Theatre. When he left school, he completed a five-year apprenticeship with the York optical instruments maker Cooke, Troughton & Simms where he stayed until 1966; he then moved to London to train at the Royal Academy of Dramatic Art. Bradley joined the Royal Shakespeare Company and performed at Laurence Olivier's National Theatre Company in the early 1970s.

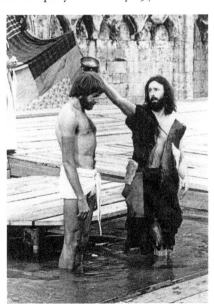

Jesus (David Bradley) baptises John. (Courtesy of the Mystery Play archive at the National College of Early Music)

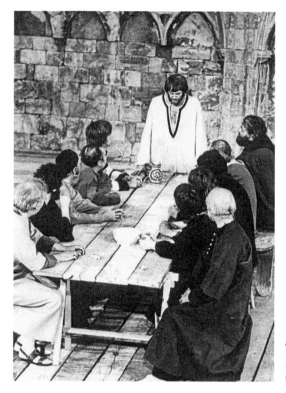

The Last Supper. (All courtesy of the
Mystery Play archive at the National
College of Early Music)

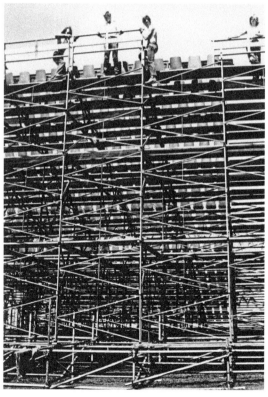

The scaffolding for the stand going up.

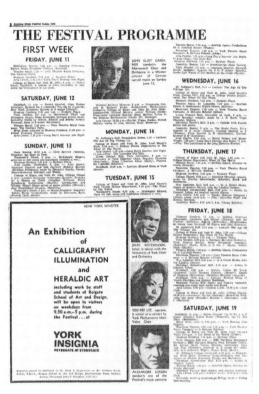

A page from the *Festival Guide* published by the *York Evening Press*.

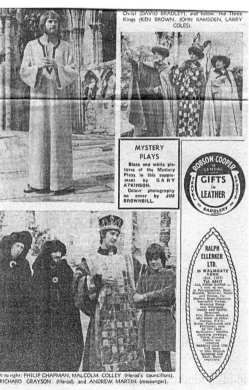

A page from *The Press* supplement.

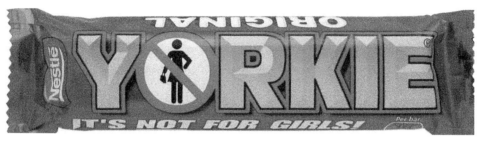

Men-only Yorkie Bar.

Yorkie Bar: *'Welcome to York ... where the men are hunky and the chocolate's chunky.'*

One of the key events in the 1970s for Rowntree was the launch of the Yorkie Bar. In 1976, Eric Nicoli identified a gap in the confectionery market and used low-price cocoa bought through Rowntree's favourable future market position to launch Yorkie. Production was at York and Norwich until 1994.

The Yorkie Bar, a chunkier, heavyweight alternative to Cadbury's Dairy Milk, was ostensibly aimed at men. In the 1980s, TV advertisements for the Yorkie Bar featured truck drivers. In 2001, the new advertising campaign made this more explicit with the slogan and wrapper tagline 'It's not for girls' illustrated by a road sign-type logo barring girls. This caused some controversy at the time, although the images and wording are still used today. Special supplies for Ministry of Defence ration packs are branded 'It's not for civvies'. In 2006, a special edition that *was* for girls was launched – in pink wrappers. If you were to arrive in or depart from York by train around fifteen years ago, you would pass a large sign that read 'Welcome to York ... where the men are hunky and the chocolate's chunky.' Truisms both.

The title to the Pet Shop Boys song 'The Truck Driver and His Mate' – b-side to the single 'Before' – was inspired by the Yorkie Bar. In the 1980s, toy lorries with the Yorkie Bar logo were manufactured by Corgi.

York Theatre Royal in 1976 – a Selection:

The Wombles Show	
Showboat (YLOS)	
Royal Ballet	
Sleuth	Anthony Shaffer
Godspell	
Oliver (YAODS)	Lionel Bart
Suite in Three Keys Noel Coward	
Syd Lawrence Orchestra	
Beckett Season (up to mid-June) includes:	
The Cocktail Party	T. S. Eliot
Scottish Opera	
A Delicate Balance	Edward Albee
In Good King Charles' Golden Days	
George Bernard Shaw	

The King's Singers (Festival)
A View from the Bridge   Arthur Miller
Creditors   August Strindberg
Larry Adler
Macbeth   William Shakespeare
Under Milk Wood Jazz Suite   Stan Tracey
The Odd Couple   Neil Simon
Hinge & Bracket
Syd Lawrence Orchestra
Under Milk Wood   Dylan Thomas
Charley's Aunt   Brandon Thomas
Mike Harding

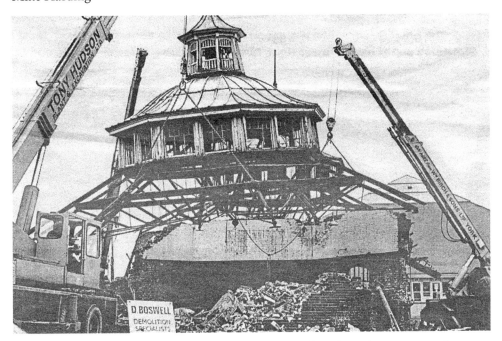

November saw the removal of the twin cupolas from the old cattle market in Paragon Street.

9

YORK IN 1977

The Queen's tour to mark twenty-five years on the throne saw her passing through Micklegate Bar again. A trumpet fanfare heralded their arrival, and the Queen and the Duke of Edinburgh went for a relaxed walkabout along a thronged Micklegate.

1977 saw the closure of York County Hospital, which had been founded in 1740 in a rented house in Monkgate and moved in 1745 to a new larger building with fifty beds on Monkgate. In the first five years of the hospital 2,417 patients were treated. In 1976 hospital facilities had moved to the New York Hospital, where there were 600 beds. The Sainsbury's supermarket at Jewbury was then built, while the hospital building, renamed County House, was converted into flats.

Jewbury was established as result of Henry II's 1177 edict that every city should have a Jewish burial ground without the city walls. It is the setting for one of York's unbelievably crass civic decisions when was proposed to lay down a memorial garden and develop the Jewish burial ground once it had been excavated by the York Archaeological Trust. Commercial venality won the day, however, and the necessities of car parking at the Foss Bank Sainsbury's prevailed over heritage, dignity and compassion. All we have to remind us now is a sorry looking plaque, easy to miss as you drive into, or walk out of, the ugliest of car parks. Sadly the York Archaeological Trust had insufficient time in which to complete the excavations on what is a key site in English Jewish history containing 475 burials.

York Theatre Royal in 1977 – a Selection:

The Amazons	Arthur Wing Pinero
Godspell	
The Glass Menagerie	Tennessee Williams
The Student Prince	
Racing Cars	
Annie Get Your Gun (YAODS)	
Diary of a Madman	Alan Drury
Margaret Clitherow	Alan Drury
Clodagh Rodgers	
John Gabriel Borkman	Henrik Ibsen
Billy Connolly	
Who's Afraid of Virginia Woolf	Edward Albee
Twelfth Night	William Shakespeare
The Winslow Boy	Terence Rattigan
Alphabetical Order	Michael Frayn
Brighouse & Rastrick Brass Band	
A Shorter Faustus	Alan Drury

10

YORK IN 1978

Colgate Palmolive Buys Terry

York, of course, was home to three major chocolate and confectionery companies in the 1970s: Rowntree Mackintosh, Craven and Terry's.

Colgate Palmolive bought Terry in 1978 for around £17 million. Although they had limited experience in confectionery through a pecan chocolate company in Texas, what they obviously lacked in knowledge of the industry they attempted to make up with in marketing expertise and experience of running a global industry. By this time, Terry's assortments accounted for around 30 per cent of the UK market with All Gold taking 20 per cent and Moonlight, the milk and plain assortment, a further 10 per cent; Rowntrees Black Magic was around 30 per cent. Colgate developed the short-lived Chocolate Lemon – a flavour they were anxious to exploit because they already used a lot of lemon in their soaps.

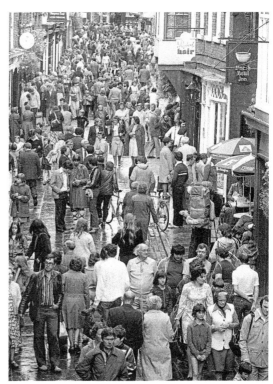

A busy Stonegate in 1978.

During the 1970s, the firm sponsored a number of races at the Knavesmire. Perhaps the most well known was the Terry's All Gold Ebor Handicap to which the firm added £10,000 in prize money, including the £600 trophy. In 1974, the famous chimney at Clementhorpe was demolished with the rest of the factory following in 1987. A vulnerable Roman mosaic was found during the demolition; Peter Terry paid for it to be excavated, and it now resides in the Yorkshire Museum. In 1975, the Bishopthorpe Road site was designated a conservation area. In 1976, Terry's launched their 56,000 cubic feet All Gold hot-air balloon, the only gold balloon in the world at that time. Apart from flights over the Knavesmire, it was also seen at Alexandra Palace and inside Olympia – the first time a hot-air balloon had been inflated inside a building. It came second in the 1978 Cross Channel Balloon race.

Joseph Terry had been making cocoa and chocolate since 1886; by the end of the 1920s, the firm had become the market leader in chocolate assortments and were building a sound reputation for producing the best in dark and bitter chocolate. The origins of the company go right back to 1767 when 'there was founded near Bootham Bar, York, a confectionery business which was destined to develop, at first into a centre where the elite of the County enjoyed their sweetmeats, and, at last after phases of success with various specialties and operation at different centres in the City, into a Chocolate Factory the name of which is recognised throughout the World as synonymous with excellence of quality.' This confectionery business was run by Messrs William Bayldon and Robert Berry.

Joseph Terry came to York from nearby Pocklington where he was born in 1793, son of a farmer, to serve an apprenticeship in apothecary in Stonegate. An advertisement in the *York Courant* in 1813 proclaims that he is established 'opposite the Castle, selling spices, pickling vinegar, essence of spruce, patent medicines and perfumery' – the usual stock in trade for an apothecary. Later, he moved this chemist's shop to Walmgate where he also practiced blood-letting using leeches, as was the usual practice. In 1823, Joseph married Harriet Atkinson, a sister-in-law of Robert Berry's; he then gave up being a chemist and druggist and joined Berry who had moved from Bootham to St Helen's Square in 1824 – the site of the first Old Factory. The front of the building was the shop (known as 'The Front Shop'), while the factory was to the rear in Brearley Yard. On offer were cakes, comfits, candied peel, marmalade, mushroom ketchup and medicated lozenges. In making this move, Joseph Terry deftly transferred from an old form of confection – a drug or pill, to the modern form – a sweet. His undoubted ability as an apothecary to 'sugar the pill' persists today with chemists selling sweets and sweet shops selling throat lozenges and the like.

George Berry succeeded his father to form the pleasantly rhyming Terry & Berry; this is how *The Yorkshire Gazette* of 29 October 1825 announced the new firm:

Joseph Terry and George Berry, confectioners, St Helen's Square, having taken the Stock and entered upon the premises of the late Robert Berry and Co, most respectfully solicit both from the Friends of the late Firm and from the Public at large, that Patronage so liberally bestowed on their Predecessors, which they will ever faithfully and anxiously endeavour to merit ... J. Terry respectfully acknowledges the very liberal Patronage bestowed upon him for the last ten years as Chemist and Druggist, in his late situation in Walmgate, and informs his friends ... that he has disposed of the stock of Drugs &c to Mr Tonge.

But George left in 1828, leaving Joseph to develop what then was essentially an expanding confectionery business.

By 1840, the railways started to facilitate transportation and, after a largely local Yorkshire distribution at first, Terry's product was being delivered to seventy-five towns all over England, including London. Products included candied eringo, coltfoot rock, pomfrets, gum balls and lozenges made from squill, camphor and horehound. Apart from boiled sweets, they also made marmalade, marzipan, mushroom ketchup and calves' jelly. Conversation lozenges, precursors of Love Hearts with such risqué slogans as 'Can you polka?', 'I want a wife', 'Do you love me?' and 'How do you flirt?', were particularly popular.

The Suspension Book of the mid-1920s makes interesting reading – suspension was, of course, unpaid, so it could be an expensive punishment: insolence, half a day; meddling with a machine, three days; packing overweight, one day; hitting a girl with a funnel, half a day; incorrectly labelling boxes, one week; leaving a handkerchief on a hot steam pipe over the lunch hour, half a day; bad piping of chocolate, five days; 'larking in the cellar', half a day; reading a newspaper, three-and-a-half days; delivering said newspaper in the van, three-and-half days; running down the yard with a bike, one day.

The famous Chocolate Orange first appeared in 1932; it had started life as Dessert Chocolate Apple in 1924 (phased out in 1954), and at one point one in ten Christmas stockings reputedly contained a Terry's Chocolate Orange. More chocolate assortments came later in the decade, including Criollo, Amazon, Dahlia, Gold Leaf, Gold Ray, Red Stripe, Sweet Thoughts and Tradition; Bridge Mints and Russian Caramels also made an appearance. Up until the Second World War, Theatre Chocolates were available with their unique rustle-proof wrappers.

During the Second World War, Terry's, in common with other chocolate manufacturers, was pressed into helping the war effort. Terry's Territorials were called up, and a fifty-person concrete shelter was built for Vine Street costing £150; at Clementhorpe, a shelter was made for 170 people in the cellar at a cost of £95, and a tunnel shelter was built at Bishopthorpe Road for 600 people to complement the 1,000 capacity ground-floor shelter, all costing £1600. Additional sandbags and steel shutters cost £3,000. Female workers were urged to train as auxiliary nurses with textbooks provided free; air-raid drills became routine.

A morale-boosting sound system was installed throughout the factory to provide 'public speech and music'; *Worker's Playtime* began at 11.30 a.m. on the BBC Home Service and was broadcast live from a factory canteen 'somewhere in Britain'. *Music while You Work* became a popular afternoon feature with hundreds of girls and women singing along together. The BBC issued stringent rules for the programme – for example, regulations that dictated what should not be played: '#1. Banned completely – all numbers with predominant rhythm, insufficient melody, or other unsuitable characteristics. #2. Banned completely – numbers that are lethargic or unsuited to any speeding up of tempo. #3. Banned completely – all modern slow waltzes, due to their soporific tendencies.' There was also a long list of specific songs that were deemed unsuitable for one reason or another, such as 'Deep in the Heart of Texas' with its clapping motif; it was felt that this would encourage workers to bang their spanners on the machinery causing damage.

Steel helmets were provided for staff. The lease on the de Grey Rooms expired and was taken over by the ATS for their physical training and by the telephone arm of the Post Office. In St Helen's Square, fire watchers patrolled on the roof, and a steel bridge was built linking Terry's with the Yorkshire Insurance company next door. After the

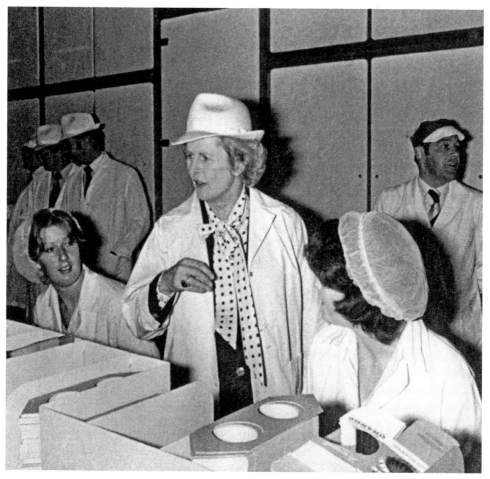

1 July 1977. *The Yorkshire Post* reported that Margaret Thatcher 'in the chocolate Neapolitan room selected one with café au lait flavour, explaining that it was "one of my favourites"'.

1942 Baedeker raid, the restaurant was unscathed and provided tea and coffee for the firemen and other rescue workers.

The tower at Terry's factory was used as a lookout post over the prisoner of war camp on nearby Knavesmire. F. Hills & Sons, manufacturers of Jablo propeller blades from Manchester, took over part of the Bishopthorpe factory to make blades and repair broken ones. Terry's staff were seconded to some of Hill's work after a period of training at Trafford Park; it often involved laminating the blades with varnish – sometimes seven days a week. Some of the bosses for the propellers were unofficially converted into biscuit barrels. Terry took over manufacturing of London firm Charbonnel & Walker's chocolate. Parts for Rolls-Royce engines were also made. Chivers & Sons occupied the Clementhorpe factory for the production of jellies, marmalades and jams until 1954 after rationing had finally ended. Freezing was done for Bird's Eye. After Chivers departed, most of Clementhorpe was given over to pastille production until that too moved to Bishopthorpe Road. During the days of rationing, employees received a monthly 'fancy order' that usually comprised one or two Chocolate Oranges and six or so bars, and an egg at Easter.

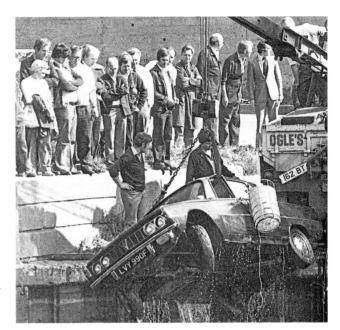

Ghoulish gawpers watching a car being fished out of the Ouse in 1978; disappointingly for them there were no bodies inside.

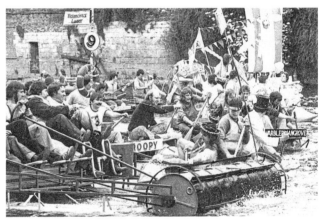

The June 1978 Raft Race on the Ouse.

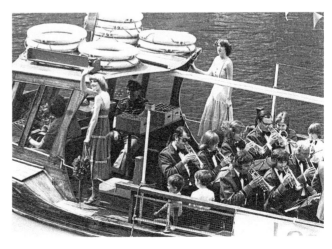

The York Railway Institute band on the Ouse in June 1978 – York's oldest brass band.

York Theatre Royal in 1978 – a Selection:

My Cousin Rachel	Daphne Du Maurier
Doctor in the House	Richard Gordon
Acker Bilk (Poppleton Sports & Social Club)	
Sleeping Prince	Terence Rattigan
Quentin Crisp	
Hair	
The Caretaker (St Peter's School)	Harold Pinter
English National Opera	
Black Dyke Mills Band	
Stephane Grappelli	
City Sugar	Stephen Poliakoff
Misalliance	George Bernard Shaw
As You Like It	William Shakespeare
Julius Caesar	William Shakespeare
Hancock's Last Half Hour	Heathcote Williams
Present Laughter	Noel Coward
Mike Harding	
King's Singers	
An Evening Without ... (Cambridge Footlights tour)	

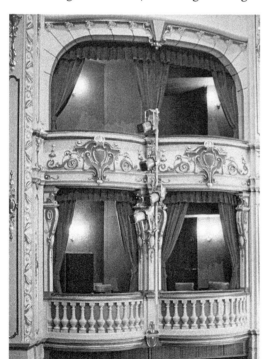

Theatre Royal boxes restored in 1978. The Civic Trust paid for the gold leaf.

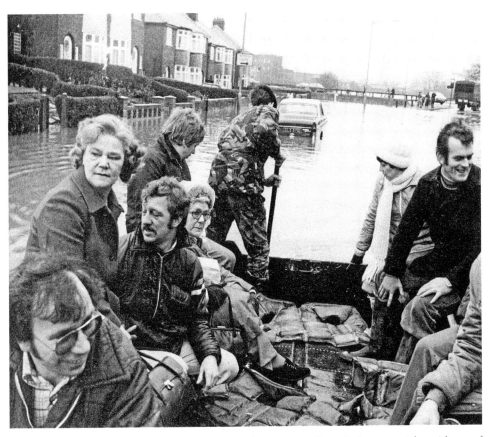

Flooding is a perennial event in York – here is the 29 December 1978 event with residents of Salisbury Road and Leeman Road being punted away by a soldier.

11

York in 1979

It was the 60th birthday of Bettys on 17 July 1979 – a day in which period music wafted through the café in York, and customers sharing the same birthday received a complimentary cup of tea and a Fat Rascal. Evidence of birthday was required by way of a driver's licence or a birth certificate. Some vintage Frederick Belmont specialties were revived, including Sarah Bernhardts, Chocolate Leopolds and Mr Belmont's Kirsch Cigar. Customers with old money could pay for their tea or coffee in pounds, shillings and pence at 1919 prices. Around 600 staff members (throughout the group) enjoyed a Diamond Jubilee Ball, and a Diamond Jubilee bonus equivalent to three months' pay.

The six exquisite Bettys are the queens of all British tearooms and they thrive in four towns in Yorkshire: two in York (St Helen's Square and Stonegate); two in Harrogate (Parliament Street and Harlow Carr); Georgian Northallerton and Ilkley. Over a million customers pass through these six doors every year.

The story of Bettys begins in September 1907 when a twenty-two-year-old Fritz Butzer arrived in England from Switzerland with no English and no idea of how to reach a town that sounded vaguely like 'Bratwurst', where a job awaited him. Fritz eventually landed up in Bradford and found work with a Swiss confectioners called Bonnet & Sons at No. 44 Darley Street. Whether Bradford was the original objective, and whether Bonnet's was the intended employer, is doubtful. In any event, they paid him the equivalent of 120 Swiss francs per month with free board. Cashing in on the fashionability of all things French, Fritz changed his name to Frederick Belmont.

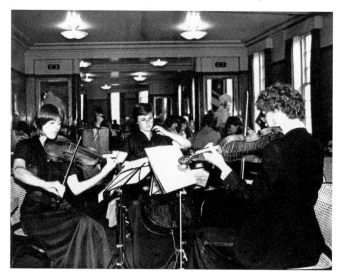

The Evening Press captured 'the quiet elegance of the Palm Court Hotel' at Bettys on 31 August 1979.

Frederick opened his first business in July 1919: a café in Cambridge Crescent on three floors fitted out to the highest standards, 'furnished in grey, with muted pink panels with old-silver borders [and] candleholders'. The china was grey-blue; the coffee and teapots heavy nickel silver. Day one takings were £30 with £220 for the first week. In 1920, he opened a second café and takings for the year were £17,000; customers included Lady Haigh, Lord Jellicoe, the Duke of Athlone and Princess Victoria.

A bakery was built in Starbeck in 1922 followed by tearooms in Bradford (in the premises of Bonnets, his first employers) in 1924, and Leeds in 1930. York opened on 1 June 1937: 'I acquired premises in York, excellent site, best in York for £25,750', Frederick tells us in his diary. York, of course, featured the famous Belmont Room based on the first-class saloon on the *Queen Mary* on whose maiden voyage Frederick and his wife Claire had sailed the previous year.

Alleged health benefits were a factor in the expansion of sales of milk chocolate in the early twentieth century, aided by claims of high nutritional values afforded by rich, pure milk content. This, of course, chimed with the traditional claims surrounding the so-called medicinal confectionery: lozenges, voice ju-jubes and barley sugar, for example, all claimed medical benefits, as indeed did Mackintosh's toffee – good for sore throats. Bettys, who produced their own chocolate for sale in their York and Harrogate cafés, tell us that sound German medical research proves that eating chocolate leads to weight loss and is beneficial in the fight against heart disease. Chocolate manufacturers' posters and advertisements of the day were populated with healthy, rubescent children and shapely women.

The true identity of Betty has never been revealed and almost certainly never will be. Speculation is rife, however, and there have been many claimants. She may have been the daughter of a doctor who practiced next door to the café and who died from tuberculosis; she could have been Betty Lupton, Queen of the Harrogate Wells from 1778 to 1838 and chief 'nymph'; she might also have been the actress Betty Fairfax who starred in the West End musical '*Betty*' around 1915 and to whom Frederick took something of a shine. Moreover, the musical toured the country and came to Harrogate's Grand Opera House three times between 1916 and 1918. Or, just as plausibly, Betty may be the name of the little girl who brought in a toy tea tray during a meeting at which the name for the new café was being discussed.

During the Second World War, Bettys stayed open and, like other cafés and restaurants, proved resourceful in making a little go a long way. Powdered egg, utility flour, corned beef, spaghetti and beans and all manner of scraps were put to good use. On one occasion, Frederick bought a lorry load of honey salvaged from a bombed warehouse and made fudge from it – a rare delicacy in wartime. Occasionally, war brides were unable to cut their cakes as the cake was nothing more than an iced over cardboard box.

On 1 February 1945, J. E. Mcdonald was the first of 600 airmen to scratch their names on the mirror at York's Bettys, known as Betty's Dive during the Second World War. Also known as Betty's Bar, it was a regular licensed haunt of the hundreds of airmen stationed in and around York; these included many Canadians from No. 6 Bomber Group. One signatory, Jim Rogers, borrowed a waitress' diamond ring to etch his name on the mirror. Many have returned to reflect on their efforts. The mirror is still on display downstairs in Bettys; many of the signatories did not survive the war.

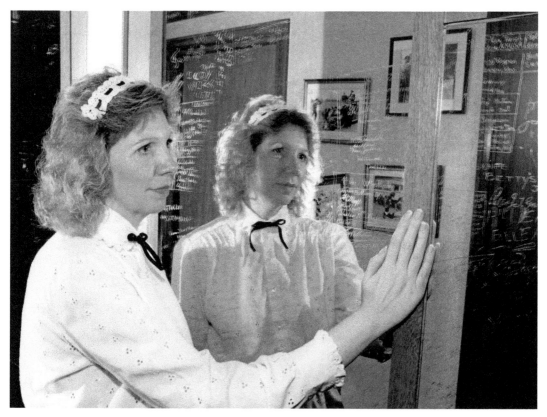

Waitress Pam Broadbent polishing the famous mirror in 1993.

Today, there are 250 staff at Bettys & Taylors handling 200,000 sacks, barrels and chests of tea every year. They buy, taste, roast pack and ship Yorkshire Tea and other special blends. They import from Sri Lanka to Japan, from Java to Ethiopia – twenty-one countries in all, in three continents. The seven buyers between them travel to all of these. The tasters, or blenders, taste up to 300 teas every day – they take five years to train and spend eighteen months abroad, six months each in Kenya, India and Sri Lanka, and six months in China. Bettys & Taylors work with the changing seasons in each of the countries because the seasons affect the crop and the taste of the tea. They work with the changing climate because rainfall, rainy seasons, and sunshine patterns fluctuate, and so does the taste of the tea. The Tropical House there is full of tea, coffee and cocoa plants – a micro-environment for Yorkshire Tea and the specialty teas from around the world.

It was Bettys & Taylors who bought the very last lot of tea at the London Tea Auction before its closure on 29 June 1998: a 44-kilo chest of Ceylon Flowery Oekoe. Taylors fought off competition from Twinings, paying £555 per kilo for the lot. The money went to charity; needless to say, it was the highest amount ever paid.

The Henry Hindley Clock Restored

Not many people know that from 1750 there was a magnificent clock over the south entrance to the Minster. It was installed by Henry Hindley to replace a ramshackle medieval clock. Henry Hindley's Striking Clock was moved to the North Transept in 1871 where it features two 400-year-old carved oak figures or 'Quarter Jacks', who strike the hours and quarters with their rods. The mechanism was moved in 1874 and all erected in its present position in 1883. In 1891, the three-minute chimes were added by Darling and Wood of York. The face and surround was redecorated in 1979, using the original design, by the Stone Yard staff. The clock has a two-second pendulum and is wound every two days. Today, the impressive clock is barely recognisable from its 1750 ancestor.

The other wonderful clock in the Minster today is the Astronomical Clock, installed in 1955 as a memorial to the Yorkshire-based Allied aircrew who flew from bases in Yorkshire and the north-east and those who died during the Second World War. One face shows the precise position of the sun in relation to the Minster at any given time while the other gives the position of the northern stars by which aircrew would have navigated. On the west side is the Zodiacal Dial representing the horizon as seen by a navigator flying south over York. Above is the inscription 'As dying and behold we live' (2 Corinthians 6.9). Above hangs the Cross and Crown of Christ in flaming gold, symbolising the supreme sacrifice and victory over loss and death.

In front of the clock there is a case containing the Roll of Honour. The names are all in alphabetical order. Spaces have been left between each letter of the alphabet filled by exact reproductions of the various aircraft flown by these airmen. Twenty-four planes are depicted – *Avro Anson, Beaufort, Whitley, Wellington, Stirling, Warwick, Sunderland, Hurricane, Battle, Typhoon, Tempest, Master, Meteor, Mosquito, Spitfire, Walrus, Blenheim, Beaufighter, Lancaster, Halifax, Tiger Moth, Lysander, Mustang* and *Catalina*. Above is inscribed, '*They went through the air and space without fear and the shining stars marked their shining deeds.*'

The 150th Anniversary of the Jonathan Martin Minster Fire

They say all things come in threes. Devastating fires at York Minster are no exception. The first was in 1829 when the arsonist Jonathan Martin destroyed the archbishop's throne, the pulpit, the organ and the choir, and damaged the choir screen and some windows. After this the Dean and Chapter prudently resolved to reinstate the lapsed post of nightwatchman. Martin was protesting against the worldliness of the church.

Jonathan Martin's fire burnt all night and was only discovered next morning when a boy called Swinbank skated by and fell over, only to see smoke pouring out of a nave window. City fire engines eventually arrived but the firemen were 'old and incapacitated ... of little use'. It took until evening and eight further engines to control the fire: the Yorkshire Insurance engine, one from the Cavalry Barracks, Beilby Thompson's from Escrick, four from Leeds and one from Tadcaster.

A second fire followed in 1840 when Leeds clockmaker William Groves left a candle burning during work and in so doing consigned the south-west tower to flames in a nine-hour furnace. Damage was extensive, destroying four floors of the tower, the roof, the peal of bells, the nave vault and roof, doors and windows. The York Operative Protestants Association were in session nearby and declared it a Catholic hoax. After this the Dean and Chapter, wincing no doubt at the combined £105,560 repair bills, resolved to insure the Minster.

The last was in 1984. UFOs and divine retribution were soon ruled out and an improvident lightning strike given as the most likely cause. Whatever, the south

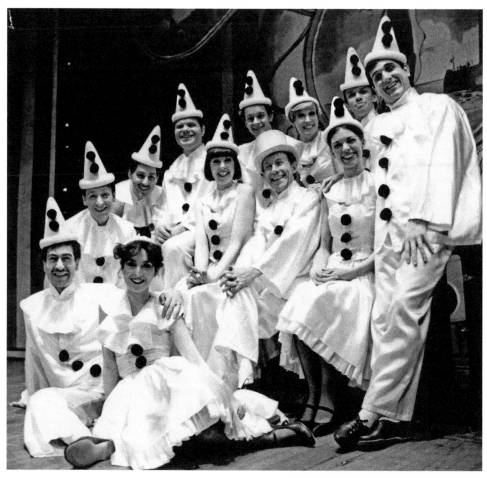

The cast of Joan Littlewood's controversial *Oh! What a Lovely War* at the Theatre Royal.

transept roof was destroyed and the beautiful Rose window shattered. Four years later, the painstaking repairs were completed, including bosses in the south transept vaulting designed by winners of a *Blue Peter* competition.

York Theatre Royal in 1979 – a Selection:

Gigi (YLOS)	Alan J. Lerner & Frederick Loewe
Oh, What a Lovely War	Joan Littlewood
Pippi Longstocking (Caricature Theatre)	
Half a Sixpence (YAODS)	
The Magistrate	A. W. Pinero
The Aspern Papers	Henry James
Witness for the Prosecution	Agatha Christie
Georgie Fame (concert presented by St John's College)	
The Taming of the Shrew	William Shakespeare
Bedroom Farce	Alan Ayckbourn

Kenny Ball's Jazz Band
(Poppleton Sports & Social Club)
Cabaret

Romeo and Juliet	William Shakespeare
She Stoops to Conquer	Oliver Goldsmith
Ruffian on the Stair	Joe Orton
Lady Windermere's Fan	Oscar Wilde
The Rocky Horror Show	Richard O'Brien
Don't Just Lie There, Say Something	Michael Pertwee
Privates on Parade	Peter Nichols

Mike Harding KOMIC KUTZ
Jasper Carrott

Websites

Borthwick Institute for Archives
www.york.ac.uk/borthwick
Fairfax House
http://www.fairfaxhouse.co.uk/
York Archaeological Trust
www.yorkarchaeology.co.uk
York Art Gallery
http://www.yorkartgallery.org.uk/Yorkshire Archaeological Society
http://www.yas.org.uk/Yorkshire Architectural and York Archaeological Society
http://www.yayas.org/
York City Archives
www.york.gov.uk/info/200424/archives/351/archives
York Civic Trust
http://www.yorkcivictrust.co.uk
York Family History Society
www.yorkfamilyhistory.org.ukYork Georgian Society
http://www.yorkgeorgiansociety.org
York Railway Museum oral history of railway men and women
www.nrm.org.uk/NRM/RailwayStories/railwayvoices.aspx

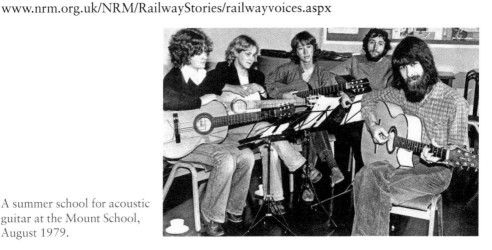

A summer school for acoustic guitar at the Mount School, August 1979.

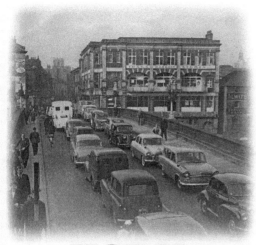

YORK
in the 1950s
Ten Years that Changed a City

PAUL CHRYSTAL

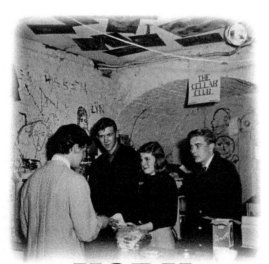

YORK
in the 1960s
Ten Years that Changed a City

PAUL CHRYSTAL

Also available…

About the Author

Paul Chrystal was educated at the universities of Hull and Southampton where he took degrees in Classics. He has worked in medical publishing for thirty-five years but now combines this with advising local visitor attractions such as the National Trust in York and York's Chocolate Story, writing features for national newspapers, as well as appearing regularly on BBC Radio and on the BBC World Service. He is the author of sixty or so books published since 2010 on a wide range of subjects, including classical history and social histories of chocolate, coffee and tea.

Related books by the author:

Chocolate: The British Chocolate Industry;
Cadbury & Fry Through Time;
York Then & Now;
History of Chocolate in York;
York A–Z;
Villages Around York Through Time;
York Places of Education Through Time;
York Industries Through Time;
Changing Scarborough;
Secret York;
The Rowntree Family of York;
In & Around York District Through Time;
Confectionery in Yorkshire Through Time;
Old Haxby & New Earswick;
Changing York;
Place Names of Yorkshire;
York's Churches and Places of Worship;
York in the 1950s;
York in the 1960s;
York & Its Railways: 1839–1950

For a complete list please visit paul.chrystal@btinternet.com

ACKNOWLEDGEMENTS

As with my books *York in the 1950s* and *York in the 1960s,* a number of the images in the book are from the superb archive of photographs held by *The Press* in York. Thanks then go out again to Steve Lewis and Perry Austin-Clarke for their generosity and the work they have done sourcing and reproducing the pictures for me. As usual, the pictures are theirs, but the captions are all mine – so any errors of fact are entirely my fault. You can see, or add to, *The Press* archive at www.press.co.uk/memories. Thanks also go to Suzy Harrison, Imagery and Digital Editor, Strategic Marketing and Digital Communications, University of York for the pictures of the University of York. Christine McDonnell at York Archaeological Trust, Sarah Sheils at the Mount School for permission to use images from her book, *Among Friends: The Story of the Mount School York* (London, 2007). John Roden was kind enough to give permission to use the Minster School photographs originally published in his *The Minster School, York: A Centenary History 1903–2004.* Last but not least, Margaret Scott, at the Mystery Play Archive, National Centre for Early Music.